Praise for **Rock-Solid Children's Ministry**

Larry Fowler's heart for children's ministry jumps off the pages of this book. Whether you have been in ministry a short time or are a children's ministry veteran, *Rock-Solid Children's Ministry* will provide you with principles that will keep your ministry grounded in Christ and focused on what matters most.

STEVE ADAMS
Children's Pastor at Saddleback Church
Lake Forest, California

Larry Fowler's latest book is one that I hope will literally "rock" your ministry. "The B.I.B.L.E." may be a song children's ministry leaders grew up singing—who wouldn't claim to "stand alone on the Word of God?"—but Larry challenges today's kid-min leaders to consider whether their ministries are truly BUILT upon a biblical model for success. He offers a biblical blueprint for ministry that will challenge, inspire and stimulate new thinking in many ministries.

KARL BASTIAN (THE KIDOLOGIST)
President and Founder, Kidology.org

Those who have been called to lead in children's ministry need to read this book! Larry's command of topics at the center of our charge are second to none. *Rock-Solid Children's Ministry* is filled with years of diverse experience and focused on God's Word. It's a must-read for the newbie and veteran alike.

MICHAEL CHANLEY
Executive Director of International Network of Children's Ministry (INCM)
Creator of CMConnect.org

In *Rock-Solid Children's Ministry*, Larry Fowler expands on his book *Rock-Solid Kids* to offer unique yet profound insights into God's design for ministry to children. I am grateful to benefit, once again, from Larry's gift of teaching and his communication of biblical truths in a way that is personal, wise and actionable. After reading this book, you will be moved, challenged and perhaps convicted—but definitely inspired—to be sure your ministry rests on the solid rock of God's Word.

CINDY CRAIG
Director of U. S. Training, Awana Clubs International

Many years ago, I read Larry Fowler's *Rock-Solid Kids*, and my ministry was forever changed. Now Larry has done it again. The concepts and topics in *Rock-Solid Children's Ministry* are thought provoking and sure to turn many children's ministries on their ear. If you are interested in sitting back and resting with a "safe" approach to children's ministry, don't read this book. Larry will spur you to action.

BRIAN DOLLAR
Founder of High Voltage Kids Ministry Resources
Author of *I Blew It!*

Larry Fowler is a leader's leader—he is rock solid. This book is chock-full of practical help and wisdom for children's ministry leaders. Everyone needs to read it!

RYAN FRANK
Executive Director of KidzMatter
Vice President of Innovation at Awana

Rock-Solid Children's Ministry will challenge both rookies and veterans to rethink and focus on their children's ministry through a solid biblical worldview. If you have a desire to grow your children's ministry with true purpose, excellence and Kingdom-focused results, this book is for you. Each chapter is packed with practical and thought-provoking topics and tools to transform the way you think, do and feel about this critical ministry. Be prepared to watch God ignite a fresh, Spirit-led passion in you and your ministry team as you read and apply the principles in this book.

KRIS SMOLL
Director of Discovery Land (Children's Ministries)
Appleton Alliance Church, Appleton, Wisconsin

Larry Fowler has hit the target once again with a compelling book that will make you reconsider how you minster to children. *Rock-Solid Children's Ministry* will inspire you and convict your heart to become more effective in your ministry.

DONNA LUCAS
Publishing Director, Gospel Light Children's Resources

Rock-Solid Children's Ministry is quite possibly Larry Fowler's best work yet and will jump to the top of the list of best books for every kidmin leader. In this complete and practical blueprint for designing an effective ministry to children, Larry clearly helps us see children's ministry from a biblical viewpoint. This is the new standard for children's ministry.

JOHN TIETSORT
National Director, eChurchDepot

LARRY FOWLER

Executive Director of Global Training for **Awana** and **KidzMatter**

ROCK-SOLID CHILDREN'S MINISTRY

Biblical Principles that will Transform Your Ministry

Regal

For more information and
special offers from Regal Books, email us at
subscribe@regalbooks.com

Published by Regal
From Gospel Light
Ventura, California, U.S.A.
www.regalbooks.com
Printed in the U.S.A.

Library of Congress Cataloging-in-Publication Data
Fowler, Larry.
Rock solid children's ministry : Biblical principles that will transform your ministry /
Larry Fowler.
p. cm
ISBN 978-0-8307-6543-0 (hard cover)
1. Church work with children. I. Title.
BV639.C4F685 2013
259'.22—dc23
2012036769

Rights for publishing this book outside the U.S.A. or in non-English languages are
administered by Gospel Light Worldwide, an international not-for-profit ministry.
For additional information, please visit www.glww.org, email info@glww.org, or write to
Gospel Light Worldwide, 1957 Eastman Avenue, Ventura, CA 93003, U.S.A.

To order copies of this book and other Regal products in bulk quantities,
please contact us at 1-800-446-7735.

CONTENTS

Section 6: Power Triangle
The Right Power in Children's Ministry

Section 7: Excellence
The Right Quality in Children's Ministry

ACKNOWLEDGMENTS

Every one of us is passing on the influence of our influencers. Through my writing, it is my privilege to extend the legacy of those who have mentored and influenced me.

Ralph Sawyer was the director of Homeward Trail Bible Camp, where many of my ministry convictions were formed. He has graduated to eternity, but I am indebted to him, as well as my parents, Mervin and Margaret Fowler, for my conviction about the priority and sufficiency of Scripture.

Jim Walters and Gil Weaver were my college professors at John Brown University and deeply impacted my thinking. Thank you, Jim and Gil, for leaving your godly imprint in my life.

Gene Goertzen, Awana missionary to southern California, has been my children's ministry mentor. He has served children for more than 50 years and is still as energetic and effective as ever. Keep going, Gene!

My co-workers Cindy Craig, Richard Yandle, Ken del Villar, Natalie Sum, Amy Staska, Diane Garmany, Tom Chilton, Betsy Sentamu and Michael Handler—who have had to put up with hearing my newest inspirations and notions during the past couple of years. You have sharpened me!

No one has had a bigger influence in my life than my wife, Diane. She is God's perfect match for me, and because she is my partner in life, my best friend and my love, I feel I am the most fortunate man in the world. Thanks, sweetheart!

FOREWORD

One question I'm asked all the time is, "Who are the churches with the best ministries to children?" That's a hard question to answer, as it all depends on how we keep score and what our definition is of a win. How do you define "good"? We know good is good and great is better, but what does it take to go from good to great? How about from same-old-same-old to effective?

I think we have been using the wrong rulers to measure success. Numbers, style, decor and even what type of check-in system we have—these all are the wrong rulers. Larry, on the other hand, is on the right page by writing a book that truly defines what I believe every person in children's ministry should be pursuing: rock-solid ministry!

You might be asking why a guy who comes from a totally different church background, ministry perspective and vantage point—one who has never had an Awana program—would be writing the foreword for this book. Good question! First of all, I'm doing it because this book isn't about doctrinal perspective, church flavor or whether you're a club person, a large-group person or a small-group person. It's about the main thing becoming the main thing in your ministry, which is our ministries becoming truly rock solid. The eight standards Larry wrote about in *Rock-Solid Kids* are game changers and provide solid biblical guidelines that every person who ministers to children needs to know and practice. Add to that the seven principles this book covers, and now we can move past theory into the practical aspects of what makes ministry effective from God's perspective.

The second reason I agreed to write the foreword is because Larry Fowler is one of the most genuine godly examples of a man of God I have ever met. Last year, Larry sought me out and asked me to forgive him and Awana for excluding my denomination during the 1980s and 1990s. I saw in Larry a heart after God and a desire for the Body of Christ to truly *be* the Body of Christ, even though some of the parts that make up that Body are different. Since then, I'm happy to say that Larry has become my friend. We have made time to hang out at every event we've both attended. I love how he leads his ministry and his family, but most of all I've gotten to see firsthand his heart for others and his heart for God. I'm honored to know him.

I love this book. The way it's divided makes it one of the best practical training tools I've ever seen. I plan to use it to train my staff and volunteers here at my church. Right thinking based on God's Word leads to right actions that produce the right outcomes in every part of our ministries, our lives and our families. Get ready to allow the Lord to take you on an incredible journey to become a rock-solid children's ministry.

Jim Wideman
Children's Ministry Pioneer
www.jimwideman.com

INTRODUCTION

Therefore everyone who hears these words of mine and puts them into practice is like a wise man who built his house on the rock.
MATTHEW 7:24

Did you ever hear the old children's song about this parable Jesus told? I learned it as a kid, and the lyrics we sang went like this:

The wise man built his house upon a rock,
The wise man built his house upon a rock,
The wise man built his house upon a rock,
And the rains came tumbling down.

The rains came down and the floods came up,
The rains came down and the floods came up,
The rains came down and the floods came up,
And the house on the rock stood firm.

We did the actions with the song, too. During this verse, we pretended that we were building by placing fist over fist. However, my friends and I were actually waiting for the big climax at the end of the second verse:

The foolish man built his house upon the sand,
The foolish man built his house upon the sand,
The foolish man built his house upon the sand,
And the rains came tumbling down.

The rains came down and the floods came up,
The rains came down and the floods came up,
The rains came down and the floods came up,
And the house on the sand went splat!

We *loved* the "splat!" The motion was one hand with palm open, facing up, and the other hand, with open palm, coming down on it. We kids would try to outdo each other making the biggest splat. It was *fun!*

The application of the third verse was, "So build your life on the Lord Jesus Christ." It was (and is) a great song. But as I've gotten older, I've learned a couple of things about it.

First, the application imagery is close to accurate, but not quite. In other passages, Jesus is the rock, and certainly it is appropriate and right to say we must build our lives on Him. However, in concluding His sermon on the mount with this parable, Jesus tells us what the rock is:

Everyone who hears these words of mine and puts them into practice is like a wise man who built his house on the rock (Matt. 7:24).

It is clear: The rock is God's Word—in this case, Jesus' teaching.

Second, we who are involved in children's ministry teach this story to children and seek to follow it ourselves in our personal lives. But maybe it has not occurred to some of us to follow it in our *ministries*.

Let me explain by telling you about the journey God started me on in the mid 1990s. I had been in children's ministry nearly 20 years and saw myself as a veteran. But at that time, the Holy Spirit began to stir my soul with this question:

What if we allowed the Bible to be the *designer* of our children's ministry?

Would it look the same, or not? I became convicted that it would not look the same, and I began searching Scripture passages that talked about children, or teaching children, for guidance.

By the early 2000s, I was teaching Scripture passages that could guide us in designing our ministry to kids. A deeper conviction continued to grow in me: God's Word must not be merely the content of children's ministry, but also the designer of children's ministry.

God's Word must not be merely the content of children's ministry, but also the designer of children's ministry.

In 2003, George Barna, founder of The Barna Group and Christian researcher of how faith and culture intersect, came to speak to the staff at my organization, Awana. He gave us a preview of his findings on children's ministry in the church, which was published later by Gospel Light under the title *Transforming Children into Spiritual Champions*. As I listened to the dismal results his research revealed, I can remember turning to someone next to me and whispering, "I just want to scream!" What I meant was, I was so stirred that I felt like standing on my chair and hollering, "Why should we expect anything different? We haven't been doing it the way the Bible says to do it!" I felt like my personal journey and Barna's research aligned, and I wanted people to see it.

I *didn't* stand on my chair and holler that day, but later, that same deep burden and emotion prompted me to write my first book, *Rock-Solid Kids.*

At the time, I observed various foundations for children's ministry: Most churches just did what they had traditionally done, with no thought as to why they were doing it. Others were more pragmatic, trying to find out for themselves what works, or copying what they observed in other churches. For those with an academic background, educational theory or child psychology was their starting point.

But the Bible was not in the mix. It was perceived as *content* for children's ministry but not as the *blueprint.* As I wrote in my introduction to *Rock-Solid Kids:*

> Children's ministry is being pushed and pulled by educational models, statistical analysis, growth techniques, cultural change and technological advancements. But with the weight of all these influences, little attention is given to what ought to be the most important influence in molding the shape of children's ministry—the Word of God. All of these other influences can be very helpful, but they should build upon scriptural truths, not the other way around.[1]

God has greatly blessed the use of *Rock-Solid Kids.* Its message has prompted some significant changes in children's ministry. In it, I set forth eight standards that ought to guide our thoughts, words and actions. They are:

Standard 1: Ministering to children is a high priority.

Standard 2: The responsibility for children's ministry first belongs to parents.

Standard 3: Scripture is the foundation of our content; relevance follows.

Standard 4: Spiritual training of children is the core lifestyle of the home.

Standard 5: Every child is safe and loved at all times.

Standard 6: Children serve God as soon as they are ready.

Standard 7: Children's workers communicate the gospel with clarity and urgency.

Standard 8: Children have regular opportunities to trust in Christ.

Since writing *Rock-Solid Kids*, my dream of its being used in Christian colleges and seminaries as a text to prepare young people for a life of service in children's ministry has been realized. I have been overwhelmed with the positive response to its message in many places around the world. Its content, in my opinion, is still foundational.

Since 2004, however, I have become persuaded that other Scripture passages ought to be considered as "designer passages" as well—ones we look to for formation of ministry. For that purpose, I am writing this book as a sequel to *Rock-Solid Kids*.

In this book, there are seven principles—one overarching principle for each of the seven sections. The table that follows lists a word for each section that describes how the section relates to children's ministry, and what the standard is that I am going to unpack in presenting the material of each section:

Section	The _____ of Children's Ministry	The Children's Ministry Standard
1	Right Target	We target the hearts of the children.
2	Right Discipline	We reflect the nature and work of God in every discipline situation.
3	Right Workers	We value both approaches—mothering and fathering—in spiritual discipleship.
4	Right Focus	We are locked on to the needs of children and the desired spiritual outcome in their lives.
5	Right Organization	We value every individual child and are concerned about not losing even one.
6	Right Power	We know where spiritual power comes from and rely upon it to fuel our ministry.
7	Right Quality	We carry out our ministry to children with biblical excellence.

Each section is divided into three parts:

- The first is a chapter that is intended to challenge you to think biblically.

- The second is a chapter that will help you think through what to do in response.

- The third is a page to address how you feel about this topic.

Why this sequence? Because I have learned a simple yet profound sequence for spiritual growth from my friend Shawn Thornton, who is the senior pastor of Calvary Community Church of Westlake Village, California. I want to pass it on to you. It is . . .

- **Think Right**
- **Do Right**
- **Feel Right**

You will learn all about this in section 1. The point is that how we *do* children's ministry is impacted primarily by how we *think* about children's ministry. In other words, *what we do follows how we think,* and how we feel is dependent upon both what we think and what we do.

I have placed discussion questions at the end of the book. It is my prayer and desire that this book will not be one that you only *read,* but rather it will be one that you *study*—with other children's ministry workers. Use the questions. Look at the Scripture passages for yourselves and learn together.

Are you ready for a journey closer to a rock-solid children's ministry? To a *Bible*-solid children's ministry? This book will guide you toward that end as you focus your attention on the rock of God's Word as the designer of your ministry with kids.

Note
1. Larry Fowler, *Rock-Solid Kids* (Ventura, CA: Gospel Light, 2004), pp. 9-10.

SECTION 1

BULL'S-EYE
The Target of Children's Ministry

STANDARD 1:
We target the hearts of the children.

Keep my commands in your heart.
PROVERBS 3:1

The eighteenth-century Dubner Maggid (literally, the preacher from Dubner, Poland), is credited with the following story:

> I was walking through the woods, and to my astonishment came upon tree after tree with a target drawn upon it. In every target, an arrow had pierced the very center of the bull's-eye. I then met a little boy with a bow in his hand. I asked him, "Did you shoot these arrows?"
>
> "Yes," he replied.
>
> Amazed that such a young boy could be such an accomplished archer, I pressed for more information: "What is your secret? How did you get to be so good as to hit the exact center every time?"
>
> "It was easy," said the boy. "I shot the arrow first and drew the target around it afterward."

Do we do that in children's ministry? Do we ever figuratively select our ministry "arrow," engage all our strength into pulling back our "bow," and then release that ministry effort without ever carefully considering where we are aiming? And then—afterward—proclaim, "It was a success!" because we drew the target after the fact?

Or do we see the target *before* our events, *before* our programs are launched, *before* we expend ministry energy? Ministry friend, you MUST start by identifying your target, and that involves answering these questions:

What is children's ministry really about?
and
What is it that we are trying to do?

TARGETING THE
HEART OF A CHILD

My friend and co-worker Ron Ryba is a serious archer. He is a member of an archery club, and he is a regular competitor in target archery. In 2011, I had the experience, along with my executive team colleagues at Awana, to receive instruction from him and try my hand at shooting a bow and arrow.

Ron started us off pretty close to the target—10 meters, I think it was—so we would have a decent chance of hitting it. I was pretty nervous—just the idea of handling something that could be deadly if aimed the wrong way was enough. Trying to protect my ego in front of my co-workers while doing something I had never done before added to the pressure.

He told us, "Try to hit the bull's-eye. You will need to experiment in order to adjust for the trajectory of the arrow. You'll need to take any breeze into account. And you'll need to get some muscle memory going so that you can pull back the string on the bow the same distance each time."

I soon learned that as a left-hander, I had to aim up and left of the target to even have a chance to hit the bull's-eye. With a number of arrows, I began to get the hang of it and even got lucky enough to hit the bull's-eye a time or two.

After a while, we urged Ron to show us how he did it. He took three arrows and went back to the 25-meter line in alignment with the far left target. He pulled back the bowstring and let go. The speed of the arrow alone produced a "wow" from us. Then we looked at the target. Bull's-eye. He took another arrow. Whish. Bull's-eye. A third: whish—bull's-eye! We were *very* impressed.

Then Ron said, "Now I'm going to those targets over there, but I'm going to do it blindfolded." He pointed to four small targets arranged as if they were on corners of a square. He took a blindfold out of his shirt pocket and put it over his eyes. Now he *really* had our interest. We watched intently as he carefully raised the bow, pulled back the string and let go. He hit the first target. "Amazing," someone said. Second arrow: second target hit. He was doing it *blindfolded. Unbelievable*, we thought. Then, the third arrow hit its target, and finally, the fourth. We never knew our co-worker had that kind of skill. Then Ron turned and faced us (his stance had kept his back toward us), and we saw his secret: a hole in the blindfold so that he could see the target with the one eye he used to aim.

He tricked us; we all had a good laugh, but it only took *some* of the amazement away. Ron was (and is) flat-out good at archery, especially compared to the rest of us.

In this chapter, we are going to talk about a different kind of target you may or may not be good at hitting. But if you haven't clarified what it is that you are aiming at, chances are you are doing a poor job of hitting anything significant.

All of us want to hit the target in ministry. But I want you to identify something more specific than the target: I want you to know what the bull's-eye is. In this chapter, I'm going to tell you what *I* name the bull's-eye. And once you understand that, it will provide a framework for the rest of the book.

So here it is: I believe the bull's-eye of children's ministry—the *center* of the target we want to hit—is the *heart* of a child. There are three reasons from Scripture for this conviction:

Why Target the Heart?

Reason #1: Close Associations

There is a close association in Scripture between the spiritual development of children and the heart. Wherever we look in the Bible to find spiritual training of children, the word "heart" is not far away. Here are some examples:

God's Word and the heart: we shouldn't separate the two, because the Bible doesn't. But sometimes we *do* in practice. Later in chapter, I will discuss this in more detail.

Wherever spiritual training is mentioned . . .	The heart is nearby:
Deuteronomy 4:9: *"Only be careful, and watch yourselves closely so that you do not forget the things your eyes have seen or let them slip from your **heart** as long as you live. **Teach** them to your children and to their children after them."*	Right in the verse!
Deuteronomy 6:7-9: *"**Impress them on your children**. Talk about them when you sit at home and when you walk along the road, when you lie down and when you get up. Tie them as symbols on your hands and bind them on your foreheads. Write them on the doorframes of your houses and on your gates."*	One verse earlier—in verse 6: "These commandments that I give you today are to be upon your hearts."
Deuteronomy 32:46: *"So that you may command your children to obey carefully all the **words of this law**."*	In the first half of the verse: "He said to them, 'Take to heart all the words I have solemnly declared to you this day."
Psalm 119:9: *"How can a young man keep his way pure? By living according to **your word**."*	Two verses later, in verse 11: "I have hidden your word in my heart that I might not sin against you."
Proverbs 3:1: *"My son, do not forget **my teaching**, but keep my commands in **your heart**."*	In the last half of the verse!
Proverbs 4:1-2: *"Listen, my sons, to a father's instruction; pay attention and gain understanding. I give you sound learning, so do not forsake **my teaching**."*	Two verses later, in verse 4: "He taught me and said, 'Lay hold of my words with all your heart; keep my commands and you will live.'"

Reason #2: The Biblical Definition of the Heart

What is the heart? Maybe it's not what you think (of course, I'm speaking of the figurative "heart," not the physical one). In our culture, we think of the heart as the core of a person, but in an emotional feeling sort of way. The huge number of heart idioms that are part of our English language is evidence of that. Here is a sample:

Heart Idioms

Where you feel	Where you find your essence	Where you think
Follow one's heart	At heart	Have a change of
Bleeding heart	Get to the heart of	heart
Broken heart	Heart of gold/stone	In one's heart of
Does my heart good	Search your heart	hearts
My heart goes out to		
Heavy heart		
Wear your heart on your sleeve		

As you can see, our usage of "heart" is lengthier on the left side of the "Heart Idiom" table. The Bible's usage is different; it would be heavier on the right side of the table. In comparison to our culture, the Bible uses the term "heart" to more often deal with one's core essence and where we think. Look at the right side of "The Three Meanings of Heart." Of course, there are many passages that talk about the mind, but I'm focusing on the usage of "heart." I want you to understand *that* term.

The Three Meanings of Heart

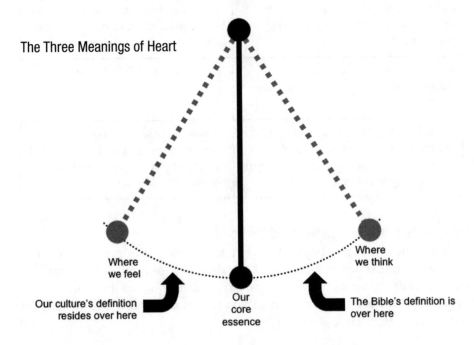

Larry Fowler

It may be helpful to understand that the heart, as used in the Bible, can be interchanged with "worldview." The Bible, however, has a different word for the center of your feelings. In both the Hebrew of the Old Testament and the Greek of the New Testament, it is the word that is literally translated "kidney." So the heart is NOT the center of feelings or emotions in most scriptural references.

I like the *New King James* translation of Proverbs 23:7: *"For as [a man] thinks in his heart, so is he."* We know that, don't we? Every action and feeling we have is preceded by thought. Jesus said as much when He proclaimed, *"A good person produces good deeds from a good heart, and an evil person produces evil deeds from an evil heart. Whatever is in your heart determines what you say"* (Luke 6:45, *NLT*).

Biblically speaking, my *heart* is where I *think*.

Do you agree? It is the HEART of a child that counts. And that (figuratively speaking) is where his or her thoughts emerge. Targeting anything less is inadequate.

I'm sure you are familiar with Psalm 119:11: *"I have hidden your word in my heart that I might not sin against you."* Proponents of Scripture memorization (I am one) often use this verse to say, "See? Scripture memory is in the Bible." Memorization of God's Word IS in the Bible, but most important, it is modeled by Jesus. The ability to recall Scripture passages or verses from memory is merely step one toward hiding God's Word in one's heart; it is not truly in a person's heart until he or she allows it to influence the way he or she *thinks*. Then it will fulfill the promise of this verse and keep that person from sin.

A final example of the Bible's usage of the *heart* is found in Deuteronomy 6:6: *"These commandments that I give you today are to be upon your hearts."* What does that mean? Does it mean that we are to have deep feelings for the commandments of God? Of course not. It means that the commandments are to guide our deep thinking, which will, in turn, result in right behavior.

Reason #3: The Bible's Pattern for Discipleship
I've already noted in the introduction that I owe the next several paragraphs to my friend Shawn Thornton, senior pastor at Calvary Community Church in Westlake Village, California. His simple yet profound

explanation of the process of growing as a disciple of Christ is based upon Philippians 4:8-9:

The Discipleship Process

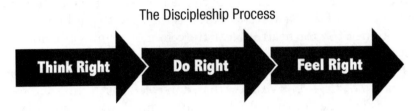

Here is the pattern in Scripture:

- First, think right: *"Finally, brothers, whatever is true, whatever is noble, whatever is right, whatever is pure, whatever is lovely, whatever is admirable—if anything is excellent or praiseworthy—think about such things"* (Phil. 4:8).
- Then, do right: *"Whatever you have learned or received or heard from me, or seen in me—put it into practice"* (v. 9a).
- Then, you will feel right: *"And the God of peace will be with you"* (v. 9b).

So, thinking right comes first. In other words, the HEART comes first—then behavior and feelings follow. If you *think* right, you will *do* right; and then, as a result, you will *feel* right. Why? Because, as Jesus said, *"For out of the overflow of the heart the mouth speaks. The good man brings good things out of the good stored up in him, and the evil man brings evil things out of the evil stored up in him"* (Matt. 12:34-35).

But we have a challenge. We are bombarded on all sides with our culture's pattern, which is exactly the reverse of Scripture. If it feels good (feels right), do it (do right); and if your thinking bothers you (like guilt or something), then adjust your thinking to the first two.

We are also barraged with behavior modification, which is better than the dominant cultural pattern. It says "do right," and if you repeat the action, thinking will eventually follow (remember Pavlov's dog?). However, behavior modification doesn't address feelings. Here are the illustrations of these two inadequate patterns:

Culture's Pattern

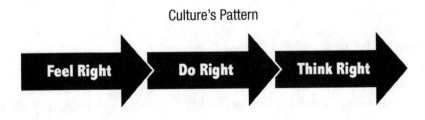

Larry Fowler

Behavior Modification

It is possible for all of us to "feel right" but not alter our thinking. Therefore, if our ministry target is to help children feel good, it is an inadequate target. However, I don't think I've ever met a children's ministry worker who would state that helping children feel good was the ultimate target.

It is also possible for a person to "do right" but not alter his or her thinking. I have done it, haven't you? Your kids do it too. Have you ever told your own children, "sit down," and they sit, but the defiant look on their face says that they are still standing up on the inside? In that case, "doing right," or changing behavior, is still inadequate because thinking has not changed.

**It is essential that we help children "think right."
When their thinking changes, their behavior—
and subsequently, their feelings—will follow.**

It is essential that we help children "think right." When their thinking changes, their behavior—and subsequently, their feelings—will follow. Biblically speaking, the heart is where they think. We *must* target the heart of a child.

Recent Children's Ministry History

Targeting the heart—and affecting it—isn't easy. Especially when we have children for only a limited time each week. The record of children's ministry over the past decades demonstrates just how difficult it is.

I am now one of the "old dogs" in children's ministry, which gives me the luxury of possessing a perspective that spans several decades. I have seen a progression of change in ministry approaches that, in my opinion, still leaves an inadequate result. I realize that the following description is a simplification, but I believe it is helpful to identify the trend.

The 1950s and 1960s

If a children's worker today saw the Sunday School material my teachers used with me when I was a child, it would probably just get tossed in the trash. First of all, there was no color; it consisted of a single half-sheet in about 9-point type with a Scripture passage on the front. There was an attempt to explain the passage in kids' terms, but I think someone just tried to simplify some adult commentary and make it work. Then there were the *questions*. They were simply regurgitate-the-facts questions that required little thinking.

There weren't many visuals. Flannelgraph was the cool new tool, but there were so few scenes and figures that it wasn't used very often. And there wasn't much thought given to environment or décor. "Just teach them God's Word" dominated the thinking of the time.

In that era, *Bible knowledge* was king of children's ministry. We were more concerned with what children *knew* than what they thought.

The 1970s and 1980s

When I graduated from John Brown University in Arkansas, I wanted to find a seminary that offered a major to prepare me for children's ministry. There was not a single graduate-level track to be found. One seminary had a youth ministry track, and two others had a Christian education track. I chose one of those and attended Talbot Seminary in Southern California.

At Talbot, there was a strong emphasis upon practical application, and I loved it. Though I was not in the pastor track, I knew that pastors were being bombarded with encouragement to make their sermons practical. As a result, there was a *huge* shift. The younger pastors were preaching differently than the older generation. Typically, the sermons were "Four [or Five, or Seven] Steps to _____." You fill in the blank.

In the Christian education division of the seminary, I was instructed to judge children's ministry lessons first and foremost by the question, "Is there a practical takeaway?" While Bible knowledge was still valued, the greatest weight was put upon what the student was to *do* as a result. We talked a lot about life change. "Horrified" was the expected response in those days to a lesson that didn't end with an application.

We also learned that the correct environment was conducive to learning, so we made sure chairs were the right size and tables faced the right way and activities were age-appropriate. We used child-appropriate décor, and flannelgraph became passé. It certainly was the age of enlightenment in children's ministry—for me, anyway!

In that era, *practical application* became king of children's ministry. We were more concerned with what children *did* than what they thought.

The 1990s and 2000s

People began to sense that children were getting bored, and a new focus emerged: our materials must be *relevant*. Practical application wasn't enough, because not every application applied to each student. Also, we didn't want children to think of the Bible as old or out of date, so we did our best to raise the cool factor and *make it relevant*. Relevance, however, was difficult to nail down. To some, it meant "don't refer to your parent*s* [emphasis on the *s*] when many of your kids have only one." To others, it meant "talk about the latest hot topic—maybe even the hottest topic of the week." And the importance of relevance spread. Publishers all proclaimed *their* curriculum to be relevant, and they put a huge marketing effort behind helping us recognize it.

We began to give themes to the décor. We all had been to Disneyland as kids, and we knew how attractive Disney was, so we began to emulate what we learned from them. We also recognized that kids are totally immersed in a technology-saturated world, so in an attempt to be *relevant*, we did the same: we improved the sound and added data projectors and big screens. Media became our delivery method of choice in an effort to stay "relevant."

In this most recent era, *relevance* has been king of children's ministry. We have been more concerned with how children *identified* with the issue than how they thought.

My Perspective of What Is Needed

Each era has had its strengths and weaknesses. In the 1950s and 1960s, we rarely thought of relevance; ministry to children could have been so much improved if we had. And what about practical application? We just left it up to the student and the parents to figure that out. In the 1970s and 1980s, Bible knowledge began to wane After all, there are just so many minutes in a lesson period, and you don't have time for everything. We hadn't really thought much about relevance yet. More recently, in the 1990s and 2000s, Bible knowledge has been in severe decline.[1]

Have we failed? Not entirely. But we haven't succeeded enough either. The overwhelming amount of research that began with George Barna's book

Ruling Emphases in Children's Ministry

1950-1970	Bible Knowledge
1970-1990	Practical Application
1990-2010	Relevance

Transforming Children into Spiritual Champions has certainly pointed that out. What has been a consistent failure in all three eras is the failure to adequately name and focus on the best target—the *heart*. While Bible knowledge is highly valuable, *knowing* Scripture does not automatically translate to changing the heart (the innermost thinking) of a child.

Practical application is also very desirable, but changing behavior can be done without a heart change. Relating Scripture in such a way that it meets a child where he or she is at is critical, but as an approach, it may fail to build a solid enough foundation to equip children for the challenges they will face later in life. So, what do we do?

We must not give up on relevance. Relevance is *a path to* heart change. We could say it is a target, but it's not the bull's-eye of the target.

We must not abandon practical application. But applying God's Word so that behavior changes may only affect the "surface" of a person. Application is part of the target, but it is not the bull's-eye. We must aim deeper.

We must not give up on Bible knowledge. God's Word is the truth, and we need to get as much truth as we can, as deep as we can, into the hearts of as many children as we can. James 4:17 says, *"Anyone, then, who knows the good he ought to do and doesn't do it, sins."* But we all agree: *knowing* isn't enough. When we focus on knowledge alone, we are missing the bull's-eye.

All three approaches have merit, but on their own they are insufficient. All three must be synergized for the best impact. And all three must be re-targeted at the bull's-eye, the heart.

The Failure of Proper Measurements

We also measure the wrong things. Suppose your big Ministry Day is over (Sunday or Wednesday, or whatever yours is), and your spouse asks, "How did it go?" You reply, "It was the best day I've ever had in ministry!" What makes you say that? Do you mean . . .

- All the volunteers showed up?
- Billy (or whoever the eight-year-old tyrant in your group is) didn't?
- You nailed the lesson?
- You actually got a compliment from a parent?
- You hit a new record in attendance?
- You heard that your pastor mentioned you (in a positive way) in the message?
- Three kids professed faith in Christ?

What is the *outcome* that makes you rejoice the most? The last one in the bulleted list is pretty awesome and certainly worth rejoicing about! Actually, all are good (well, maybe not the one about Billy), but none are the best measurement. Even counting children who profess faith in Christ is not the best, because we really don't know their heart decision.

We must intentionally target the heart. Maybe you are saying in response, "Well, Larry, I DO target the heart." Great. Do you hit it? In other words, are you *changing the way children think*?

"But it is so difficult to know whether we are doing that or not," you protest. Of *course*; that is the nature of children's ministry. It is one huge differentiating factor between business and ministry; in business, the bottom line is very measurable—did we make money or not? In ministry, the essence of what we do is to impact the immeasurable—the heart of a person. "Are we training the heart?" is similar to asking, "Am I becoming more Christlike?" I can't measure it with real accuracy, but I *can* know whether there is progress or not, and I *can* know what it takes to get there. Let's take the same approach with training the hearts of children.

Responding to the Crisis

I am certain you are aware of the crisis we are in: We have well-documented research that our children are abandoning their faith-walk in unacceptable numbers. Too many of our children have excelled in "head knowledge" of Scripture but then walk away from their faith. Others have learned the "Christian way" to behave, but their hearts don't follow. And many of our children have enjoyed children's ministry with its more recent coolness factor, yet they are ill-equipped to battle competing messages.

We *have* to do better. We have changed over the last half-century, and we must learn from the failures of the past and change even more. I believe it will be the hardest change yet for children's ministry.

Let's be biblical. Let's target the hearts of the children we serve. Now we need to understand how to do that, which is the subject of the next chapter.

Note

1. In a small research project (2007) in which I participated, we asked 100 Bible colleges and seminaries two questions: (1) "Do you measure the Bible knowledge of incoming freshmen?" and, (2) if so, "Have you seen any trends?" While few measured, most had an opinion. Many responded like this: "The general consensus of the Bible and theology faculty is that there has been a marked

decrease in the level of Bible knowledge in recent years" (Toccoa Falls College); "General Bible knowledge has been steadily declining over the past 10 years based on the Bible Content Entrance Test" (Briarcrest College and Seminary); and "The level of Bible knowledge for our incoming students has decreased dramatically over the last 20 years. Our assumption now is that incoming freshmen know nothing about the Bible, and that we must start at the most basic level" (Puget Sound Christian College).

SEVEN WAYS TO IMPACT THINKING

What impacts the heart?

When I ask people that question, the answers I've heard are usually vague and sometimes incorrect, because we all tend to think of answers that are in line with the cultural meaning of "heart" instead of the biblical meaning. To clarify what I am wanting, I ask instead, "What impacts thinking?" Since we can usually identify what has impacted our thinking, we can identify those principles that can guide us in children's ministry.

The ability to impact thinking is not dependent upon what curriculum you use or whether you use media in your delivery. It is not dependent upon organization or programming. Your budget doesn't matter—and neither do your facilities. So, what does impacting the heart depend upon? Here are seven behaviors the Holy Spirit can use to affect the hearts of our kids, no matter our church size or our role or our ministry budget or skill sets.

Modeling

Can the children in my ministry see a godly Christian life lived out in front of them by someone they know and trust?

More than any other single factor, modeling molds thinking. In particular, the modeling of someone *with whom there is a strong relationship* influences thinking. In fact, the stronger the relationship, the more impactful the modeling is.

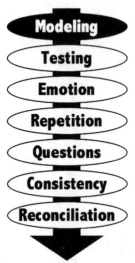

Modeling
Testing
Emotion
Repetition
Questions
Consistency
Reconciliation

What "modeling" am I talking about? Put simply, it is *an observable example of godliness.* There are two parts to this.

First, it has to be observable, because if it is not observable, it is not modeling. Children need to *see* us live the Christian life, not just *hear* us say they should live the Christian life. Parental involvement in the spiritual training of children is so important because parents are the most observable by kids and they have the strongest relationship; therefore, a parent's example packs the greatest power.

Second, it must be an example of godliness. If it is another example, it is still modeling, but it is the wrong kind.

If it is true that modeling is the single greatest factor for influencing thinking (and it is), there are huge implications for ministering to children in the church as well. This factor needs to impact every role:

- *Teacher, see your role differently.* Teachers are not communicators of content, but rather mentors and models. You never teach a lesson; you always teach a child! You are the shepherd, and the children are your sheep. Your job is to lead them—and lead them well.

- *Group leaders, build strong, godly relationships with the children assigned to you, and then show them how to live for God.* Remember, shepherds know their sheep. It goes without saying that the better you know them, the stronger your relationship will be.

- *Directors, resist the temptation to rotate teachers or assign them for short periods of time.* It is simply not possible to build adequate, impactful relationships once a month. Rotating teachers is also not good for the teacher; it usually results in their seeing the role as "filling a slot," not as mentoring and modeling.

- *Directors, organize in such a way that modeling is possible.* That means small groups must be small—a volunteer cannot maintain a strong godly relationship with more than five or six children. We will discuss this in more depth in section 2.

- *Leaders, become storytellers—especially tellers of personal stories of faith and God at work.* Tell them your testimony. Relate your experiences verbally. Then children will be able to "see" your model of faith.

Teachers, don't teach a lesson; they teach a child.

Testing

Are children in my ministry given opportunities to exercise and test their faith?

By testing, I mean "seeing if it works." Your thinking can be *quickly* altered through a test. So can a child's. You can tell a toddler over and over again, "Don't touch the stove, because it is hot," and that child will still reach out to try to touch it. But if his little fingers get burned, his thinking will be quickly altered. Of course, since in some cases (the stove is a good example), we don't want them to learn this way, we won't use this method to validate everything we tell them.

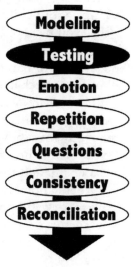

How do we encourage children to test their faith? We are really good at telling them, and they may be able to repeat back what we have told them, but their thinking may not change unless they can test it. Do you ever challenge your children to try what you've told them? "Try praying—and see what happens." "Try honoring your mom—and see if it changes things in your home." This emphasis is especially important in middle elementary years—when they are just beginning to enter the age of life where they will determine if their faith is their own.

My good friend Karl Bastian, who is the founder and president of Kidology, relates this story about his son "testing" what he was told:

> My son just graduated from Pre-K at a Christian school, and they gave all the kids a medal with a character trait. We were proud that Luke's medal said "Faith." The teacher shared a story of a time this year when Luke lost his beloved stuffed dog, Charlie. The class prayed it would be found and Luke said, "I know I'll get my dog back, because I prayed, and God answers prayer." We had searched

everywhere and given up. (We did not know he had asked the class to pray!) The next day, I remembered he had taken it into Chick-fil-A a week earlier. I went in during a hunch and asked, and a manager said, "We find lots of toys and can't save them all, but this one just seemed so loved I decided to hang on to it!" When I returned it to Luke, only then did he tell us his class had been praying and he had faith God would help us find Charlie. When Luke walked into class the next day with Charlie, the teacher burst into tears because she had been fervently praying privately that God would answer my son's prayer and affirm his young faith!

I find Karl's final comment about the teacher interesting. She is like all of us—a little worried that if we have kids "test" their faith, it might not turn out the way we want. But if we are going to impact their hearts, we must risk it anyway.

Teachers, challenge your students rather than tell them. Suppose you are teaching about children honoring their parents. Don't just *tell* them to do it (the "you need to honor your mom and dad" approach), but challenge them to test it: "Kids, give it one week—see if God's Word works. Speak and act to your parents in a way that honors them for one week, and then tell me next week if you like the result."

Directors, create events, outings and opportunities that allow faith to be exercised. Let your kids serve in children's ministry. Some children's pastors are getting more adventurous, and I applaud them: They let their 11- and 12-year-olds (who are thinking they are too mature for VBS) participate in leadership and then, as a team, go run a VBS in another community.

Others allow the children who demonstrate sincerity in faith and a desire to serve fill positions right within children's ministry. In fact, they allow them to participate alongside all the adult workers—even in teaching lessons, planning the calendar and things normally reserved for the key leaders.

Emotion

Are children in my ministry observing and experiencing positive emotions about following Christ?

In the previous chapter, I said that feelings don't come first—but that doesn't mean they aren't an important consideration. Emotion has been called "the highway to the heart." Because fathers are so influential on a child's faith, I often ask grown-ups questions about their own father's impact on them. One of my favorite questions is, "Did your father cry?" When I ask that in a group setting, like a workshop, there is always someone in the room that says "Only once." When I get that response, I ask, "Was it memorable to you?" And the answer is always, "Of course." And the reason for the dad's tears is readily recalled. Emotion can leave a huge impact.

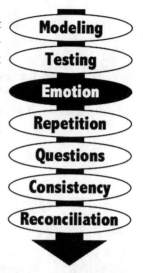

Have you noticed that dads are very successful at passing on their sports values? Whether it is loyalty to their favorite team or a liking for a certain sport or pastime, few fail to win over their children. I can say (with a little pride, I might add) that I have been successful in that. My primary loyalty, sportswise, is to the Nebraska Cornhuskers (college football), because I grew up there. My children and my grandchildren, who have never lived in Nebraska or even close to there, are all Husker fans. Why? Because they have seen my emotions when it comes to that team. They've seen me yell at the TV and scream and holler. They know I don't do that as often with other things. Emotions are simply powerful.

How about emotion over spiritual things? Have my kids and grandkids also seen me get excited about God's Word? Have they seen me get passionate about sharing my faith? About grieving over the spiritual needs of neighbors? Fortunately, I can say yes. But I wish I could say that I have displayed those emotions more often than I have.

The bottom line is that godly modeling and emotions tied together produce a powerful impact on a child's thinking.

We usually have it backward in children's ministry. We do a lot to get children emotional (usually that means excited), but real impact comes when the adult leader is genuinely emotional about spiritual things.

- Do you ever let your personal excitement over a particular truth in Scripture show? We often show excitement when a child learns a verse or a truth, but what is our excitement really about? Is it about their achievement (that's okay), or is our excitement about God's Word itself?
- Do you ever let your grief over others' sin be seen? That's a lot better than simply berating the sinner.
- Do you ever reveal your remorse over your own sin?

- Do you ever show your joy over a child's faith in Christ?
- How in awe of God are you in the presence of children?

Think about these areas and pick one that you can genuinely demonstrate in front of the children the next time you minister. Watch their reaction, and see if you have a greater impact. I am sure you will.

Repetition

Are children in my ministry challenged to regularly review, remember and repeat core Bible truths and concepts?

Repetition impacts thinking. Remember back to elementary school, and how you repeated and repeated the math tables until you had them memorized? Why was there so much repetition? So that you could just *think* that 7 plus 9 equals 16—you didn't need to calculate it out. Repetition enables thinking mathematically. It will also enable thinking spiritually, but we had better be intentional about it.

Earlier in this chapter, I discussed the weakness of children's ministry during the 1950s and 1960s, which focused only on Bible knowledge. Knowing Bible facts and truths is not entirely worthless—in fact, it is extremely valuable. It is just not the bull's-eye part of the target.

Kris Smoll, director of children's ministry at Appleton Alliance Church in Wisconsin, has taken the think right/do right/feel right concept and applied it to the teaching approach throughout their children's ministry. But she has also improved it, because she put a fourth goal in front: know right. She understands that knowledge is preparatory for thinking, but knowledge of a truth rarely impacts thinking through a one-time exposure; it only has that effect when it is repeated and reviewed over time.

Systematic repetition of core truths will also affect how a child thinks over time. More and more, I hear of congregations that are not on the "high church" side of Christianity, but they include something in their children's ministry structure that resembles a catechism. Why? Because we recognize that repeating key concepts will have a positive impact over time.

Larry Fowler

Recently, my wife, Diane, and I had the privilege to become acquainted with Summer Christopher. She is the director of Pipeline, the children's ministry at Sandals Church in Riverside, California. Sandals is a young mega-church that God has blessed with rapid growth and amazing outreach. The words "not traditional" only begin to describe its approach. In our conversation, Summer described their curriculum for Pipeline by saying, "It's kind of a catechism." It struck me as paradoxical—a church that is nontraditional in almost every way using a catechism-like approach to learning. Summer gets it—repetition of key truths can have a great impact. She went on to explain her approach:

> I have done a great deal of research toward the classical approach to education. The premise of this form of education is based on the developmental abilities of elementary-aged children to take in vast amounts of information, whether they are capable of fully understanding it or not. Then they have it committed to memory for the rest of their lives, ready to access when needed.
>
> I have seen huge successes in the classroom and in church as kindergarteners through sixth graders have committed to memory information such as the Periodic Table of Elements, all 50 states and their capitals, the Christmas story verbatim based on Luke 2, the entire book of Philippians and much more. I could talk about this all day.
>
> One thing we have learned about this stage of learning is that once information is received during this period, it often stays with us for the rest of our lives. Just think about how much school knowledge, etiquette, or even useless TV jingles you learned as a child and can recall even today!
>
> What we are working on now is more of a question/answer approach that takes students throughout the Bible, giving them anchors to hold on to as they obtain more and more Bible knowledge and encounter the living God. These anchors point them to the central Person of the Bible, that of a real Savior who redeems His people.

In my ministry (Awana), we have also stressed repetition. We are not afraid of large amounts of content, but we want to see that it is retained. So we have deliberately increased review of key concepts and Bible verses, and the repetition is not just within a week, or a year; rather, it is over multiple years so that we are doing all we can to enable children to deeply instill biblical truth into their knowledge base.

What does this mean? If we want to impact the thinking of a child, we will be intentional about identifying key truths and returning to them many times so that they will be driven deep into the spiritual knowledge foundations of the children that God entrusts to us. We are not trying to make "talking parrots" out of the children. This is not about rote or mechanical answers; it is about acting on our awareness that repetition is critical for long-term impact.

Teachers, here are some practical ideas for including repetition into your children's ministry:

- Make time for review, every week, of what was taught the previous week. In addition, review every quarter of what was taught the previous quarter, and review every year what was taught the previous year. Of course, this means that your volunteers have to be tuned in to the bigger picture of scope and sequence—and also that you keep it the same over a longer period of time.

- What do you review? For certain, review verses and concepts that have to do with the nature of God, the truthfulness of His Word and the work of His Son. There is nothing more foundational to a person's thinking than his or her view of God. So why wouldn't we be faithful in reviewing that more than anything else?

- Make the décor in your rooms communicate the key concepts to be reviewed in each group.

What if you are not the teacher? Then support the teacher by reviewing his or her lesson with the children you are working with (and do it with genuine, positive emotion). Do so, and you will greatly enhance the spiritual impact on the hearts of the children!

Questions
Are children in my ministry challenged to think and given opportunity to express their thoughts and questions?

We must discipline ourselves to become question askers. All too often, we are advice givers and truth tellers, and those roles are vital. However, if we miss the opportunity to be question askers, we miss the opportunity to better impact the heart. If deep questions linger in the thinking of kids, how will we know how to address them if we don't bring them out?

Why ask questions? For two connected reasons:

1. So that you will know what the children are thinking.
2. So that you will know how to better impact what they are thinking.

That means we must create *opportunities* in our children's ministry for asking questions. That is another reason to make sure there are *small* (five to six kids) small groups.

Asking questions should pervade every age level. It doesn't start with older elementary (though abstract questions might); it starts with the two-year-olds. Teachers and leaders should be asking "how," "why," "what if" and "what do you think" questions appropriate for each age level.

So, how do you know if your questions are good? By observing what kind of answers they give back. Are they simply recalling facts, or do their answers demonstrate that they are *thinking*? Here's a question to ask that provides a great test: "Do my questions result in their questions?"

You *can* do this—no matter what your position in children's ministry! Let me encourage you to experiment. The next time you are with the children in a teaching session (whether you are the one teaching or not) think of two or three questions you can ask the children afterward—either as a group or individually. Remember, the questions must be . . .

- How?
- Why?
- What if?
- What do you think?

Consistency

Are the children receiving the same message concerning the gospel and how to be a Christ-follower from all the workers in my ministry?

When presenting the content of this chapter in a workshop, I am frequently asked, "Isn't consistency almost the same as repetition?" I answer "No, not at all." There are three parts to consistency:

1. *Consistency among influencers.* This means that children receive the same message from various influential sources. This is

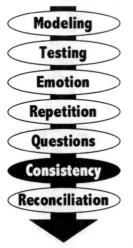

especially critical *when one should expect that the message would be the same.* Here's what I mean: *Christian* parents should be giving a child the *same* messages that children's ministry workers at church give. One would expect that. One would not expect that non-Christian parents would give the same message. However, when children's workers at church send one message to children (for example, "prayer is important") but Christian parents send another (they never pray), a child's thinking about prayer is confused at best.

2. *Consistency over time.* Parents who punish for something one time but let it go another time violate the important principle of consistency and mess with the minds of their children. What are the children supposed to think? It's also critical in church. Children's ministry leaders must provide oversight to see that their workers don't give conflicting messages either verbally or nonverbally, or else the children will be confused.

3. *Consistency between words and actions.* Need I say more? When we don't practice what we preach, or in the case of children's workers, take on what we teach, we will not effectively impact the hearts of children for God.

Remember that while you can't control the other influencers in a child's life, you can model consistency before him or her in what you do. Be responsible for *you.*

Reconciliation
Are workers in my ministry mirroring both the holiness and the love of God when there is a need to discipline a child?

Whenever discipline is required with an individual child, there is a huge opportunity to impact that child's thinking. I can't think of anything that can cement a child's view of God more than completing the process of discipline with reconciliation.

Disobedience by a child provides a potent learning opportunity. How we respond with discipline provides a make-it-or-break-it teaching moment, and when the whole issue/event is completed with reconciliation, we have maybe the best opportunity put before us to impact a child's image of, and thinking about, God.

That is all I will say about this point now. You'll learn a whole lot more in the next section.

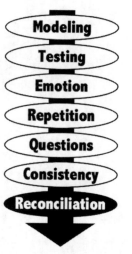

*　*　*　*　*

Target the *heart*. Make that your bull's-eye. *Change* thinking. Do so, and you will impact a child for life.

THANK GOD FOR HEART IMPACT

"Ralph Sawyer.
  Abe Penner.
  James Walters.
  Mervin and Margaret Fowler.
  Gil Weaver.
  Art Rorheim.
  Gene Goertzen.
  Thank You, God, for these wonderful servants of Yours who have deeply impacted the way I think—and especially thank You for my mom and dad and their close walk with you that molded my heart."

Now you do the same—take a minute and feel right. Write down the names of those people who molded your heart for the things of God. Then thank Him for each one.

Do something else: Think of an opportunity you have had to impact the heart—the *thinking*—of those in your family, your ministry and your world. Tell yourself, *God, you used me to impact [that person]'s heart. Thanks!* Rest in the peace that comes from being in a position to be used by the Holy Spirit.

Feel right.

Larry Fowler

SECTION 2

RECONCILIATION
Discipline in Children's Ministry

STANDARD 2:
We reflect the nature and work of God in every discipline situation.

The Lord disciplines those he loves, and he punishes everyone he accepts as a son.
HEBREWS 12:6

The most opportune time to teach children what God is like is not in a lesson or a small group discussion or a nature walk or worship experience. Instead:

The most opportune time to teach children about the nature of God is when you discipline.

When a child does something wrong, you can either reflect God through how you handle it, or you can—by your actions and response—instill in the child a wrong view of God.

The stakes are high. Emotions (at least on the part of the child) are often showing, relationships might be teetering, and the results can be long-reaching. The learning—whatever it is—may become deeply embedded in the child's heart.

In this section, you will learn the major elements of God's discipline system for us. I pray that you will be deeply challenged not only in your role as a children's worker, but also in your role as a parent to use the same model to guide your discipline of those God has given into your care.

GOD'S ECONOMY OF DISCIPLINE

God's process of discipline is revealed again and again in the Bible. His dealing with the children of Israel is a recurrent theme throughout the Old Testament. In the New Testament, we learn the need for and the significance of Jesus' death on the cross in payment for our sins.

There are six major elements in God's economy, or system, of discipline. Three elements are God's, two elements are man's, and one is the result that is initiated by God. In this section, I am going to build a model that describes His economy, or system, of discipline one element at a time.

God's Economy of Discipline

Element 1: God Made the Rules

We call them the "Law." By the Law, God established His standard of righteousness and provided a means to know when something is right or wrong—in other words, when it is sin.

Element 2: When We Sin . . .

We are all aware that the Bible teaches the sinful nature of man. We read it in many passages, such as these from Romans 3:

As it is written: "There is no one righteous, not even one; there is no one who understands, no one who seeks God. All have turned away, they have together become worthless; there is no one who does good, not even one" (vv. 10-12).

For all have sinned and fall short of the glory of God (v. 23).

We are also aware that sin has consequences—the most critical one is that it breaks a person's relationship with God:

But your iniquities have separated you from your God; your sins have hidden his face from you, so that he will not hear (Isa. 59:2).

The separation from God that results from sin is not only a present relational reality but is also an eternal consequence, as we read in Romans 6:

For the wages of sin is death, but the gift of God is eternal life in Christ Jesus our Lord (Rom. 6:23).

I assume that you already know this. It's likely you have taught it to kids many, many times. But I want to also remind you about what doesn't have consequences. I love Romans 8:38-39, because it is a passage that gives us believers a list of what won't separate us from God:

For I am convinced that neither death nor life, neither angels nor demons, neither the present nor the future, nor any powers, neither height nor depth, nor anything else in all creation, will be able to separate us from the love of God that is in Christ Jesus our Lord.

If Paul had written this passage just for children's workers, though, it might have looked something like this:

For I am convinced that neither loudness nor shyness, neither odors nor dirt, neither culture nor color, nor immaturity, neither goofiness nor ADHD, nor any other obnoxious peculiarity, will be able to separate us from the love of God that is in Christ Jesus our Lord.

What is the point? ONLY SIN separates from God. NOTHING else! Yet, *we* distance ourselves from other people for all sorts of reasons (including those mentioned above). Aren't you thankful that God is not like us? And if we want to reflect Christ when there is a "discipline opportunity," we must be careful to do the same.

God's Economy of Discipline

Element 3: When We Sin, God Punishes . . .

I want you to take note of three things in this section.

1. Punishment Is *Always* the Consequence of Sin

In God's economy of discipline, *punishment is ALWAYS the consequence of sin*— 100 percent of the time. Paul wrote, *"Anyone who does wrong will be repaid for his wrong, and there is no favoritism"* (Col. 3:25). Sin NEVER goes without punishment. Sometimes God may choose to extend grace and remove the punishment from us. After all, what is Christ's death on the cross but the payment of our *punishment.* The fact that our sin is paid for in His death only underscores that punishment is the result of sin.

Two characteristics of God are so important to remember here: the holiness of God and the love of God. Interestingly, we are told to emulate God in both of these areas:

> *But just as he who called you is holy, so be holy in all you do; for it is written: "Be holy, because I am holy"* (1 Pet. 1:15-16).

> *This is love: not that we loved God, but that he loved us and sent his Son as an atoning sacrifice for our sins. Dear friends, since God so loved us, we also ought to love one another* (1 John 4:10-11).

Several years ago, I had the experience of sitting next to a lady for the long flight from Los Angeles to Sydney, Australia. She described her beliefs as New Age and viewed sitting next to me as a perfect opportunity to try to convert me away from the "horrors" of believing in sin, punishment and hell. She was so repulsed by the idea that I recall she said something like, "How can you believe that a loving God can send anyone to eternity in hell? I refuse to believe in that kind of a God."

I asked a question: "Is it loving to allow sin to go unpunished?" She didn't answer my question. "I just think God forgives people," she said.

I responded to her with a question she wasn't expecting: "What other character qualities of God do you believe in?" She listed several but didn't mention "holy."

So I asked her: "How about holy?"

"Well, yes, 'holy' too," she responded.

I kept going. "Will heaven be holy? Will there be sin there?"

"Of course it will be holy. There will be no sin."

"Let me ask a different question. If I steal a watch from a store, am I a thief?"

She couldn't tell where I was going with this, and I could see that bothered her. "Yes . . . you are a thief."

"Suppose that a year later I haven't been caught, and neither have I taken the watch back. Am I still a thief?"

"Yes." She was uneasy.

"Suppose I get caught, get sentenced and serve my time. Once I get out of jail, am I still a thief?"

She had to think. "No, I guess not . . ."

"So, if I sin, but the sin goes unpunished, I'm still a sinner, right?"

"Yes, I suppose so . . ." She was clearly feeling nervous.

"But you just said that there was no sin in heaven. In order for there to be no sin in heaven, the sins of those who go there have to be paid for, don't they? If the punishment of sinners is not paid, then everyone who goes there is still a sinner, and then there is sin in heaven."

I'm not sure I persuaded her of anything, but I can confidently say she didn't accomplish her goal of recruiting me!

2. God Never Punishes for That Which Is Not Sin

God never punishes for immaturity or personality traits. He never punishes just because He is tired or has a lot of pressures at work, or any of the reasons we end up using. That is *not* to say that God does not have consequences for immaturity or foolish decisions or ignorance or weakness. He often allows serious faith-building experiences for those He loves.

One of the most meaningful passages in the Bible for me personally is 2 Corinthians 12:9-10, in which Paul writes, *"But he said to me, 'My grace is sufficient for you, for my power is made perfect in weakness.' Therefore I will boast all the more gladly about my weaknesses, so that Christ's power may rest on me. That is why, for Christ's sake, I delight in weaknesses, in insults, in hardships, in persecutions, in difficulties. For when I am weak, then I am strong."*

I have learned that I mature the most when life is the most difficult. I have *learned* it (you probably have too), but God knew it *all along*. That is why He allows consequences and struggles, but they are frequently not punishment for sin.

The effect of *sin*, however, is *punishment*.

Figuring this out is a lot easier for God than it is for you and me. God has the decided advantage, because He can discern our motives and our thoughts. When we are in the role of disciplinarian, we can't always know whether the child's behavior is sin or not.

3. Punishment Always Has a Purpose

God never punishes in order to retaliate. He doesn't do it to vent or express His anger. He doesn't transfer His wrath (He doesn't take it out on us because something else is not going well for Him . . . if that were possible). He only does it for one purpose, and that is to produce element 4:

God's Economy of Discipline

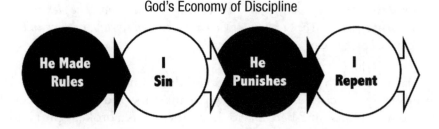

Element 4: God Punishes So that We Will Repent

You've seen it—you are in the grocery store checkout line, and a toddler is pitching a whale of a fit because he or she can't get the candy by the checkout counter. After a few minutes of trying to ignore the bloodcurdling screams, mom reaches the Limit of Tolerance and yells back, through gritted teeth, and accompanied by a look that could kill. The toddler either screams even louder or else—in case her approach works—begins sniffling back into silence. Mom continues the process of paying for her groceries.

In that scenario, the objective of mom is not repentance, but simply behavior modification. In other words, she just wants the tantrum to stop; and when it does, she goes on with her activity.

I'm persuaded that parents punish like that way too often, but God NEVER does. His purpose is always clear—it's for our *repentance*. In God's economy of discipline, there is ALWAYS a purpose in punishment, and the purpose is always the same—it is always for our repentance.

What Is Repentance?

Nave's Topical Bible has probably been my favorite source for studying Scripture over my ministry career (now I do it online). "Repentance" is defined there as "a complete reversal of one's attitude and values." My friend Dave Pearson illustrates it for kids this way.[1] He starts walking one direction on the stage, repeating, "I'm doing things my way, I'm doing things my way, I'm doing things—" Then he stops, does a 180-degree turn, and starts walking the other direction, repeating, "I'm doing things God's way, I'm doing things God's way . . ."

Repentance is heart change. It is not simply a change in behavior. If we think God is done with us when we say "I'm sorry" but have full intentions of doing the sin again, we will discover differently.

King David knew this. Psalm 51 is his expression of repentance for his sin with Bathsheba and Uriah. He says in verses 16 and 17:

> *You do not delight in sacrifice, or I would bring it; you do not take pleasure in burnt offerings. The sacrifices of God are a broken spirit; a broken and contrite heart, O God, you will not despise.*

David knew what God wanted. God didn't punish so that he, David, would bring a sacrifice. That is how pagans appeased their gods. God wanted repentance, and here David describes that as a broken spirit and a broken and contrite heart.

That is God's intent. It is His target. His reason for punishing. We must mirror His purpose when we discipline, whether it is in our homes or in our classrooms.

God's Economy of Discipline

He Made Rules → I Sin → He Punishes → I Repent → He Forgives

Larry Fowler

Element 5: When We Repent, God Forgives

He forgives every time. Notice the progression in 2 Chronicles 7:14:

If my people, who are called by my name, will humble themselves and pray and seek my face and turn from their wicked ways, then will I hear from heaven and will forgive their sin and will heal their land.

In this verse, repentance is indicated by the process of *"humble themselves and pray and seek my face and turn."* God responds by "hear, forgive and heal." We have one incredible God! I have to confess, I don't always forgive so well. I sometimes hold a grudge, and I too often remember a wrong. But God is different:

- God forgives *completely*: *"If we confess our sins, he is faithful and just and will forgive us our sins and purify us from **all unrighteousness**"* (1 John 1:9, emphasis added).

- God forgives *unconditionally*. There's no "if" in God's forgiveness.

- God not only forgives, He *forgets*. Here is just one example of the many passages that tell us this awesome truth: *"I, even I, am he who blots out your transgressions, for my own sake, and remembers your sins no more"* (Isa. 43:25).

Do you see? God responds to repentance with *forgiveness*. We are now in position to go to the final element in God's economy of discipline: reconciliation.

God's Economy of Discipline

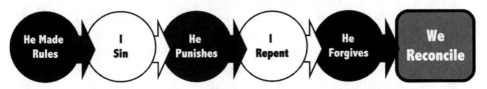

Element 6: When We Have Repented, and God Has Forgiven, He Reconciles Us

Reconcile. I think there is no more beautiful word in the Bible.

I got off the airplane, and upon walking into the gate area I could hear a large crowd down a couple of gates. As I got closer, I could see that a large group of military families were waiting for their loved ones to return from duty. There were little boys holding signs scrawled in their own handwriting, "Welcome home, Dad."

A little girl was going up and down on her tiptoes, her gaze riveted on the Jetway door. Her sign said, "Hug me first!" There were moms of the children, dressed in their finest, hair and makeup carefully done because they were about to see their husbands and lovers for the first time in quite a while. There were young men holding bouquets of flowers, and there were single girls and elderly parents—all waiting for their family members or boyfriends or girlfriends to appear. Many of us from the other gate area had stopped because we knew the sight we were about to witness would be special—and it was.

Then the Jetway door opened.

Immediately there was almost a holy hush of anticipation. The first soldier stepped out. The crowd erupted into cheering and applause, except for one family. They didn't have time to applaud—they went running into his arms. There were shrieks, tears, hugs and jumping up and down from extreme joy.

But there was no time to enjoy watching that reunion, because a young man with the flowers was next to be reunited. Then there was another reunion, then another. I saw the dad of the little girl with the sign appear, and she did get the first hug! I couldn't help it—my eyes welled with tears of joy along with the families. I could see that a number of the other onlookers were wiping away tears as well. We lingered until most of the families were reunited, and then we went on to pick up our luggage. "Wow, that was something," I said to another passenger. "It sure was," were the only words he could say. I could see he was still struggling to control the emotions of the moment.

That was a reunion! The reuniting of loved ones after an extended absence is a beautiful thing. Reunions happen when people meet again after being physically apart. But what is better than a reunion—and more beautiful as well—is *reconciliation*. Reconciliation happens when we are spiritually reunited after being apart.

What is reconciliation? It is restoring a relationship to what it was before it was broken. Reconciliation can be as simple as a toddler crawling up on mom's lap for a hug, or it can be *so* difficult when there is deep hurt. In that case, the offender must humble himself or herself to the point of brokenness, and the person offended must extend unconditional forgiveness. In either case, it is an incredible picture of our God and His ministry to us.

Our One-word Ministry

Reconciliation is what we are called to do in children's ministry. In fact, this single word is a summary of *any* ministry, whether it is reconciling a sinner to a relationship with God, reconciling a believer to the image of Christ, reconciling people with one another or reconciling our society to God's intention. The apostle Paul wrote:

> *Therefore, if anyone is in Christ, he is a new creation; the old has gone, the new has come! All this is from God, who reconciled us to himself through Christ and gave us the ministry of reconciliation: that God was reconciling the world to himself in Christ, not counting men's sins against them. And he has committed to us the message of reconciliation. We are therefore Christ's ambassadors, as though God were making his appeal through us* (2 Cor. 5:17-20).

Notice that believers have been given both the ministry and the message of reconciliation. And that applies not only to adult ministry, but it certainly describes the ministry and message of those who work with kids as well!

"But," you protest, "'reconciliation' is such a BIG word!" Exactly. And so we need to be able to help children understand it. An instance of discipline gives us the perfect opportunity.

Let's move to how "God's Economy of Discipline" can guide us in the discipline issues we face with kids. In the next chapter, I'm going to reference how it ought to impact both parents and children's workers.

Note

1. Dave is the director of Children's and Family Ministry at Medinah Baptist Church in Medinah, Illinois.

MIRRORING GOD IN DISCIPLINE

"We've Got a Discipline Problem . . ."

Has a co-worker ever said that to you? Your internal response was probably a big groan. You *dread* having to deal with a discipline problem. Have you also said it yourself? I have. I have faced many "discipline issues" in ministry.

Susie was the first. As a young youth pastor in a small church, I felt baffled as I tried to figure out how to handle her. She would come into our Sunday morning youth group and do everything she could to stay uninvolved in the direction I wanted the group to go. She would pass notes, whisper to whoever was next to her, roll her eyes and generate a chilly response to nearly everything spiritual.

Billy was next—smelly, dirty, uncombed hair, loud and hyper. He was desperate for attention, and he had learned somewhere that he could get it by disrupting whatever was going on.

Richard and Ben had had a fight at school, and they brought it to church. I walked into the boys' bathroom to find Richard sitting on top of Ben, banging his head on the floor.

Angus had his plan about where he wanted to sit, and any child who wanted his chair would get bullied into moving if we, the leaders, weren't watching.

Max would totally check out, playing with his imaginary friends instead of engaging in the lesson.

Kyler was athletic, good-looking and loved the girls' attention—and he would do just about anything to get it.

These are the names of some of the kids who have been my biggest challenges in discipline. I fear that I didn't handle some of them very well.

I didn't ever figure Susie out.

With Billy, insight into a home where dad abandoned the family, where mom worked two jobs, and Billy and his brother and sister fended for themselves helped me understand. Diane and I did everything we could to love them and help them cope. After a couple of years, they moved, and we lost contact.

I broke up Richard and Ben's fight, but Richard never came back. If the truth be known, I didn't like him, so I never bothered to follow up. I needed to read section 5, "The Significant 'One.'" Of course, I hadn't written it yet.

What do you do with the difficult discipline problems you face? Handling the child who challenges rules and boundaries can be a huge dilemma for children's workers. Do you allow one child to continue in the group when there is a strong possibility that the others will be distracted to the point of not learning? I'm not going to give you the specifics of what to do in this chapter; instead, I want you to think about implementing a *system*—one that mirrors God's system.

Incomplete Instructions

I've spent lots of years training children's workers about discipline. I've taught workshops and probably coached hundreds of people. During my ministry career, I have also evaluated more than 1,000 children's ministries—some with great control of kids, and some with no control. Here's the summary of what I have taught, either in a classroom setting or in a consultation:

- *You need clear rules, or expectations.* Not too many—and word them positively—but you do need rules.

- *You need to know what to do if the rules are violated.* In other words, spell out the consequences: time out, and so on, including taking them to their parents.

- *You need to discern between crowd control and individual rebellion.* You need to have separate techniques to deal with each.

　　　　Larry Fowler

All of these actions are part of our training in Awana. I knew them well, but they didn't help in the following instance: I was serving as a small group leader in the Awana club in my church. I had eight boys in my group, and we were meeting around an 8-foot table. I was sitting on one of the long sides, near the end. Two of the boys were first-timers, and they were sitting at the end nearest me. I was talking with them, getting acquainted, when a commotion from the other end interrupted our conversation. The two boys there, one Hispanic and one Asian, had started teasing each other, and one threw in a racial insult. The other retaliated with one of his own, and just that quick, they were ready to start throwing punches.

I knew exactly what to do. After all—we have clear guidelines about such incidents in Awana, and I teach them—so I was ready.

I evaluated the situation: This was not a case of crowd control but of individual misbehavior—*serious* misbehavior. Tempers were out of control, and the situation needed to be handled quickly and privately.

Our discipline plan was clear—in such cases, the director is to remove the misbehaving kids from the group, calm them down and deal with them in a more private setting.

So, I called the director over and told him the situation while I kept the two boys somewhat separated from each other, and I let him handle it.

I did my part, but it didn't end well. The director took the two boys out into the hallway and verbally blasted them for their behavior. They came back to the group but were sullen and uncooperative. I tried to reengage them but failed. That meeting was the last time I saw them. Both of them were from unsupportive homes, and so the choice to come was probably theirs and theirs alone. And they decided to never come back.

What went wrong? I thought I was following the process, and I think the club director felt he was too. But something was missing—badly missing—from how we handled it. As a result, we lost two kids.

I've done a lot of soul-searching since that incident several years ago. I've discovered that simply getting the how-to's down and establishing a behavior correction system isn't enough. So that is where we are going to go in this chapter. If you want the techniques and practical advice, I know you can find other sources.

I want to do something different: I want to give you a model to follow that will help you reflect Christ when you discipline. Let me repeat what I said on the introductory page of this section:

The most opportune time to teach children about the nature of God is when you discipline.

High Stakes

There is no single event in children's ministry when the stakes are higher than when there is an opportunity to discipline.

The stakes are high for *teachers and leaders*. We are pretty good at appearing godly when we are up in front of the kids, but let a child lose *his or her* temper and our temper is tempted to follow. One instance of losing our cool can destroy our ability to minister, at least with the child that is on the receiving end.

The stakes are even higher for the children involved. Their emotions are front and center. Egos are fragile, and they are vulnerable. A wrong approach can leave them hurt, bitter or angry—and, like the two boys in my story, they might never come back.

The seriousness of a wrong approach is seen in Jesus' proclamation in Matthew 18:6:

> *But if anyone causes one of these little ones who believe in me to sin, it would be better for him to have a large millstone hung around his neck and to be drowned in the depths of the sea.*

The high stakes mean that we have to approach a discipline situation with the greatest caution. But it also means we can view these times as the greatest opportunities to teach—especially to teach about the nature of God . . . *if* we use the model of God's Economy of Discipline to guide us in dealing with discipline opportunities and apply the model to our role as an authority over children.

God-based Discipline

Here is the model we are going to follow:

My God-Based Discipline Model

As you can see by the diagram, we (as either a parent or a children's worker) represent God in the discipline opportunity.

Element 1: Rules

In the home, making the rules and enforcing them is the responsibility of the parent, of course; at church, it is the responsibility of the ministry leader. If you are not that person who makes the rules, you are to support the enforcement of them.

It is important in children's ministry to differentiate between guidelines that inform children about group order and attention, and rules concerning individual issues. In ministry, there needs to be just a few guidelines and rules, positively stated, with a system in place to guide enforcement of the rules.

Element 2: A Child Sins

It happens all the time in the home and pretty regularly in children's ministry: a child acts inappropriately. The very first question we must ask is, "Is this sin?" In other words, "Is it a willful act of disobedience?" There are three possible answers:

1. *No.* We determine that our toddler was just tired. The burp coming from one of the kids in the back row of our large group time was unintended. Do we punish? Definitely not. That doesn't mean we do not allow consequences to come into play, but the consequence is not punishment. For example, Ethan (one of the boys in a small group near mine) is easily distracted. A consequence his teacher can use is to isolate him for short periods of time in a setting where he can concentrate, but that is not punishment—it is simply a consequence of Ethan's being unable to focus with other kids around him. A tired toddler may be put to bed, but not as punishment, because rest is exactly the consequence that is needed.

2. *Maybe*—we don't know. Do we punish if we are not sure? Definitely not. God doesn't have to be concerned with this option. He ALWAYS knows if what we are doing or thinking is sin. But we aren't God, so often we don't know. In this case, we must err toward the "no" side. We are not going to punish unless we are sure it is willful disobedience.

3. *Yes.* We must represent God and administer punishment. Obviously, for children's workers, our options for methods

of punishment are quite limited because we are not the parent. Nevertheless, we can administer punishment for sin if it follows within policy guidelines set forth by the ministry leadership, and if parents have given us permission to do so. If both of those things are not true, it is probably best to inform the parents of the sin and allow them to do the disciplining.

The first step in following God's model is simple but difficult: We must discipline ourselves to ask, "Is this sin?" It is easier for parents to discern because they know their own child well. It is much more difficult for children's workers to determine; therefore, they must exercise caution in administering punishment to an individual child.

Element 3: I Punish

Punishment is NEVER appropriate when the action or attitude of the child is not sin. If what the child did is not sin, but punishment is administered anyway:

- It is simply and purely child abuse. There may be degrees of severity, but the fact remains, it is abuse.

- It can instill a deep fear and distrust of authority in the child.

- It will damage the child's ability to understand God accurately. If a father is guilty of punishment for things that are not sin, there is a high probability that the child will be fearful of both the father *and* God.

However, punishment IS the appropriate response when the child does sin. I believe failure to punish for sinful behavior is a form of child abuse as well.

Tony (not his real name) is an acquaintance of mine. I've observed him more than once dealing with his young elementary-age daughter when she has disobeyed. He will tell her what the punishment is going to be, or start the lecture, and immediately she starts saying, "I've got a tummy ache" or "I have to go to the bathroom."

The second statement really works well on dad, and Tony lets her go. Of course she stays in the bathroom for a long time—because when she comes out, Tony's resolve to discipline her has pretty much evaporated. She usually gets a warning, and the discipline is over. Unfortunately, Tony is also teaching his daughter something about authority that is harmful to her development as a person.

Children's worker, you are dealing with many kids who experience less-than-ideal discipline tactics at home. What an opportunity for you to minister! They may be abused—receiving punishment for things that are not sin—and you are the only one in their world who will mirror how God deals with sin. But you may also have children who have no boundaries. With them you have the awesome privilege of helping them understand that God has limits and you do too.

How do you see the misbehavior of a child? As an irritation? As something that ruins your good plans for a lesson? Or as an opportunity to demonstrate in real life what the character and work of God is like?

Element 4: The Child Repents

I wrote previously that one of the greatest failures of recent generations of parents and children's workers is the practice of behavior modification. "If we just get them to behave well we think our job is getting done. But like teaching, correcting sinful behavior must ultimately reach the heart or else it has limited effectiveness at best.

Of the five elements, correction is also the one we most often neglect. Why? Because it takes so much time and is often so inconvenient.

Let's pause in describing the elements and consider a scenario. Bianca had her three kids in the backseat as she headed to the grocery store. There were only 20 minutes to get groceries before she had to get Amanda and Alicia, the seven-year-old twins, to soccer. Tony, the five-year-old, began grossing out his sisters by trying to make bubbles with his saliva. He was in boy heaven—they were screaming, "Mom, make him stop! He's spitting on us!" The more they screamed, the more he slobbered. Bianca said, "Tony, stop. What you're doing is bothering your sisters."

After about the third warning, she'd had more than enough. She swerved to the side of the street and braked to a quick stop.

"TO-NY!" His mother's facial expression and tone of voice told him it was now time to listen to mom. "STOP, or I'll leave you in the car all by yourself while I get groceries!" Bianca knew she wouldn't do that, but she had to threaten something. Fortunately, it was enough: Tony stopped—for a few minutes. Then, as they were pulling into a space in the store parking lot, he did it again. "Tony, get out of the car!" Bianca knew they had to hurry to make the soccer practice. She ignored his behavior, put him in a cart and all four of them went into the store to get groceries.

What did Bianca do that was wrong?

- She didn't identify the sin. Making bubbles with saliva wasn't the sin—he was just being a little brother. But not stopping when she told him to stop *was* sin.

- She didn't punish the sin. She threatened punishment, but her threat was unenforceable, and she knew it when she said it.

- She didn't get Tony to a point of repentance. He was likely still thinking about how fun it was to get such a reaction from his big sisters.

By contrast to how Bianca did it, we must always be consistent in discipline *and* pursue repentance. This also means we must never punish in anger. Why? Because when you are angry, you have conflicted motives. You may be hurt, and punishment may have revenge as its aim. You may be irritated, and punishment will help you feel vindicated.

"Sorry" isn't enough. Many of us teach our children to say "I'm sorry" as the response to punishment. But saying that is adequate only when it is an expression of repentance. Saying the words "I'm sorry" can mean "I'm sorry I got caught" or "I know this is what I must say to get out of this situation."

When *is* a child repentant?

- When the child understands that what he or she did was wrong.
- When the child agrees to ask for forgiveness from God and those offended and make it right.
- When the child desires to not do it again.

You can usually tell this when the child will simply but sincerely say three things:

"I sinned."

"I don't want to do it again."

"I want to be forgiven for what I have done."

It is really good to encourage the child to first pray those things to God—because every sin is a sin against Him. Then, if it is a sin against another person, be willing to say those things to that person as well.

So, how *do* you get a child to repent if he or she is still defiant after punishment?

- Make sure the child understands that his or her repentance is the goal.

- *Don't* do it by heaping on more punishment.
- Spend *time* talking over the three points above (what he did was wrong, he needs to make it right, and he doesn't want to do it again).

This can be *so* inconvenient. In the home, it can mean postponing plans, delaying dinner, turning off the TV and a host of other inopportune things. In children's ministry it can mean others taking over so the person dealing with the child can minister properly. It can mean abandoning lesson plans and changing activities—but all are essential if we are to deal with discipline issues properly.

Element 5: I Forgive

Often, it is not just me that must forgive. It must also be the person who was sinned against—another kid, for example. In that case, the offending child needs to be ready to ask for forgiveness (that is a part of being repentant) from the one he or she hurt.

It is so helpful to teach the child to say, "I was wrong. I sinned against you. Will you forgive me?"

Remember, too, that our forgiveness must mirror God's. Like He does with us, we must . . .

Forgive *completely*.

Forgive *unconditionally*. There's no "if" in God's forgiveness, so there can be no "if" in ours.

Forgive and *forget*. We can't bring it up again later. *"As far as the east is from the west,"* (Ps. 103:12) God removes our sin when He forgives. We need to do the same with kids!

God taught me a great lesson on a warm Friday (warm for Chicago) in mid-March. I was anxious to get in my first round of golf, so I took the afternoon off from work to go play on a course that had just opened for the spring season.

I asked the guy at the pro shop if I could play by myself and also play two balls, not just one (I wanted to get the practice in), and he said I could because the course was pretty empty. So I got a cart and took off. The first few holes were so enjoyable—I could play at my own pace because no one was with me and no one was pushing me. There was a twosome ahead of me and a foursome ahead of them. I just hung back so I could play at a leisurely pace.

Then I saw another single golfer finishing the hole behind me. *Where did he come from?* I wondered. A short while later, I had just finished putting on the fifth green when I heard a thud not far away—it was the golfer's ball. He had caught up and had hit the ball *while I was still putting.* I was ticked. No, I was TICKED. I drove my cart on over to the next tee where the twosome was waiting to tee off, seething all the way.

"Do you want to play through?" they asked. "No," I responded. "I want to just play slowly by myself." Then I added, "But the guy behind me might want to—he appears to be in a big hurry. Did you see he hit his ball on the green while I was still there?" I was hoping to get him off my heels.

They went ahead and hit their golf balls and took off, which left me sitting alone by the tee. Wouldn't you know it, the golfer behind me finished and came rushing right up and parked his cart right behind mine. I tried to ignore him, but it didn't work: "Do you mind if I join up with you?" he asked. That was the *last* thing I wanted. I wanted to play by myself, and I was still mad at him. "No, you just go ahead and play through. The twosome up ahead will let you play through too. You're in a hurry—just go ahead, because I want to take my time." I was trying to hide my irritation.

"Oh, I'm not in any hurry. I'll just play with you." *What, not in a hurry?* I didn't believe it. "Well, you sure were on that last hole. You about hit me while I was still on the green."

"Oh, did I? I'm so sorry. I didn't realize . . . hey, I'm really sorry."

It sounded real sincere, but I wasn't done being mad at him. "It's all right," I lied. "No big deal."

He pulled his cart up beside mine. He *was* going to play with me . . . and just like that, my Ideal Day had just turned into Torture Day. Then this guy, in his early twenties, had the audacity to try to start conversation: "So what do you do for a living?"

Now I had to either lie or admit who I was. This time, I didn't lie: "I work with a Christian children and youth ministry." I was stuck. Now I was going to have to *act* like a Christian. He lit up.

"Really? Which one?"

Great. Now he's gonna be able to identify me later. I'm going to have to at least act like I forgive him for spoiling my day. "Awana."

"Wow, I'm an Awana leader in my church! I went to it as a kid and now I work in it." He was so pumped that we had that connection. I faked enthusiasm, but inside I was still seething.

We had small talk for a while, but after a couple of holes my conscience really began to bother me: I hadn't forgiven him. He had sincerely offered an apology, but I was so upset because my agenda had been altered that I hadn't forgiven him. The Holy Spirit really began to convict me, but I wasn't about to give in. My game went south because I couldn't concentrate.

It was finally on the fifteenth hole that I knew I was wrong. I said, "Hey, Joe (actually, I've forgotten his name), I have something I need to say. Remember back on the fifth hole when you joined me? You asked me to forgive you, and I said I did, but I didn't. I've been kind of mad the whole way. I am asking you to forgive me for not forgiving you." He did, and relief came over me. My golf game didn't get any better the last few holes, but I surely felt better inside.

With Joe, I didn't forgive. I said the words, but I didn't mean them. I hung on to my bitterness too long. We can do the same as parents or as children's workers with the children we minister to—but God never does. He forgives completely and unconditionally, and He *forgets*.

Element 6: We Reconcile
Remember what reconciliation is: restoring a relationship to what it was before it was broken. You have to get all the way there! Don't stop short! Complete the circle!

What Does Reconciliation Look Like?
For Joe and me, it was just another handshake that let each of us know the issue was forgotten.

For a young child, it may simply be a minute or two of cuddling. For a teenage boy, it may be a slap on the back or maybe some humor. It may be expressed through "Let's get a bowl of ice cream," and then you change the subject while you eat.

In families, it needs to regularly include eye-to-eye contact and the words, "I love you with all my heart."

In children's ministry, I'd do it this way: "Trevor, let's get back with the group. Wanna sit by me?" The last phrase says "the relationship is restored." That is *so* critical.

Who Initiates Reconciliation?
Usually, the authority does. That is the parent in the home and the children's worker at church. The child is not likely to do it, so the parent or leader must. The authority is responsible to make sure the discipline cycle is completed.

* * * * *

Children's worker, you can do this! You can follow God's pattern in discipline. When you do, you will teach a lesson with more power than any visual aid, object lesson or story. The next time a child misbehaves, think of the pattern that God sets in dealing with sin and seek to follow it. You—and the child—will be so glad you did.

RESTORE A RELATIONSHIP

Have you overlooked completing the reconciliation process with some-one—at sometime or other? How about with your own children? Have you reconciled? How about a child you disciplined in your ministry? Have you reconciled?

If you've identified either someone or a situation that needs attention, think about all the positives that might come from initiating reconcilia-tion. Then do it.

Here's what I have wanted you to learn in this section:

- Think like God thinks about the discipline process.

- Follow His example in what you do to discipline your own child or a child in your ministry.

- Feel the joy of a restored relationship. It is one awesome feeling, isn't it?

SECTION 3

GENDER BALANCE
The Workers of Children's Ministry

STANDARD 3:
We value both approaches—mothering and fathering—
in spiritual discipleship.

We were gentle among you, like a mother. . . . We dealt with each of you as a father.
1 THESSALONIANS 2:7,11

Does it make any difference who serves in children's ministry? As long as a person is committed to Christ, and serving well, does it really matter? I believe it does—and I believe it is time we actively gave attention to bringing a better balance to who serves. In this section, you will learn that there is an imbalance, and there is a biblical foundation for seeing more equal representation between men and women in children's ministry.

Does it make any difference? My friend Michael Chanley, the executive director of the International Network of Children's Ministry, would also say yes—based upon his personal experience as a boy. Michael says:

> The first time I heard the gospel message presented to me as an invitation was when I was 11 or 12 years old. It was at VBS, and the little old lady (older than my grandparents) told me I had to make a choice between giving all of my life to God or none of it . . . it was an all or nothing decision. I told her I would think about it. Later that night I remember deciding that God would have to wait. I wanted to have fun like my friends were doing.
>
> My decision was based on my experience at church. What I saw at church was that 80 percent to 90 percent were women, and older than my grandparents. And in my boyish perspective, accepting Christ represented two things I was not interested in becoming: old and feminine. I'm still not interested in doing either of those things, though I can only control one of them.
>
> I accepted Christ 10 years later, as a U.S. Marine.

What? Reject Christ simply because of the gender of a children's worker? Does it really matter that much to kids? You will see that it does—not just from the perspective of a little boy, but also from the perspective of all children—*and from Scripture.*

FATHERLESSNESS IN THE CHURCH

We Need More Men!

Please don't misunderstand—I am not proposing in any shape or form that we need less from women; instead, I want to help you see how critical it is that we get more from men in children's ministry.

We Need Men in Our Homes

We could use more constructive male involvement in a lot of places, couldn't we? Of course, that need is most clearly seen in the home. Dr. Matt Daniels, founder of Alliance for Marriage™, summarizes it this way:

> *Our homes—and therefore our communities—can benefit from better fathering.* Research now shows that the percentage of fatherless families in a community more reliably predicts that community's rate of violent crime than any other factor, including race. The same can be said for rates of child poverty.[1]

Every societal ill is exacerbated by the absence of fatherly influence in the home. In his book *Fatherless America,* David Blankenhorn makes this bold statement:

In the United States at the close of the twentieth century, paternal disinvestment has become the major cause of declining child well-being and the underlying source of our most important social problems, especially those rooted in violence.[2]

Here are two examples of societal issues that Mr. Blankenhorn cites as rooted in fatherlessness:

1. *Youth violence.* "There are exceptions, of course, but here is the rule: Boys raised by traditionally masculine fathers generally do not commit crimes. Fatherless boys commit crimes."[3]

2. *Child sexual abuse.* Blankenhorn proposes, "Child abuse is a terrible crime, regardless of the identity or family status of the perpetrator . . . but a child is sexually safer with her father than she is with any other man. . . . She is also safer with a father than without one."[4]

The devastation that accompanies fatherlessness in our communities is well documented by hundreds, perhaps thousands, of sources. The list is long: domestic violence, child poverty, adolescent childbearing and economic insecurity are four others that Mr. Blankenhorn identifies. It is not my intent to delve deeper—we know that it is a societal pandemic that is out of control in our culture.

We Need Men in Our Churches

Our churches can benefit from better fathering. Male involvement in our churches, whether in simple attendance or in service is vital to the health of our congregations. I appreciate the analysis of English vicar Robbie Low on the issue of fathers' influence on church attendance:

In 1994, the Swiss carried out an extra survey that the researchers for our masters in Europe (I write from England) were happy to record. The question was asked to determine whether a person's religion carried through to the next generation, and if so, why, or if not, why not. The result is dynamite. There is one critical factor. It is overwhelming, and it is this: It is the religious practice of the father of the family that, above all, determines the future attendance at or absence from church of the children.

If both father and mother attend regularly, 33 percent of their children will end up as regular churchgoers, and 41 percent will end up attending irregularly. Only a quarter of their children will end up not practicing at all. If the father is irregular and mother regular, only 3 percent of the children will subsequently become regulars themselves, while a further 59 percent will become irregulars. Thirty-eight percent will be lost.

If the father is non-practicing and mother regular, only 2 percent of children will become regular worshippers, and 37 percent will attend irregularly. Over 60 percent of their children will be lost completely to the church.

Let us look at the figures the other way round. What happens if the father is regular but the mother irregular or non-practicing? Extraordinarily, the percentage of children becoming regular goes *up* from 33 percent to 38 percent with the irregular mother and to 44 percent with the non-practicing, as if loyalty to father's commitment grows in proportion to mother's laxity, indifference, or hostility.

Even when the father is an irregular attender there are some extraordinary effects. An irregular father and a non-practicing mother will yield 25 percent of their children as regular attenders in their future life and a further 23 percent as irregulars. This is *twelve times* the yield where the roles are reversed.

Where neither parent practices, to nobody's very great surprise, only 4 percent of children will become regular attendees and 15 percent irregulars. Eighty percent will be lost to the faith.[5]

Affects of Parent's Attendence

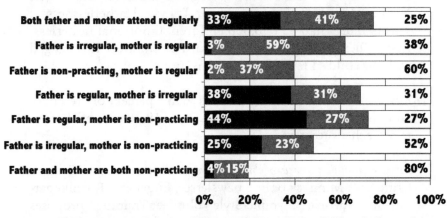

If the impact of the father is so critical to church attendance, is it unfair to assume that an absence of fathering influence is also critical in the ministries of the church? I don't think so.

Is this an issue worth talking about and doing something about? I hope to persuade you that it is.

The Dangerous Imbalance

I am part of a minority. As a middle-class male of European descent in America, my minority status is not connected to my ethnicity or my social stratum, but rather to my lifelong participation in working with kids. As a male—a "more mature" male—I am not only a minority but part of a "super-minority." The world of those who influence kids is hugely out of balance—and it is an unacceptable, untenable situation. Here are some facts:

- *Men are a minority of attendees in the church.* Various polls and surveys show that a large majority of church attendees are women. I believe no one is happy about the lack of male involvement; however, it is interesting to me that all the remedies proposed are related to what you do to attract adult men, not what you can do while those men are boys.

- *Men who are involved significantly with their own children are a minority.* More than one-half of the children in America will spend a significant part of their childhood without a father present in their life. The results are devastating and well documented. The National Center for Fathering states, "physical fatherlessness . . . affects more than 25,000,000 children. Emotional fatherlessness—when dad is in the home but not emotionally engaged with his child's life—affects millions more.[6]

- *Men are a minority in our schools.* Less than 3 percent of preschool and kindergarten teachers are men; only 19 percent of elementary teachers are men.[7]

- *Men are a small minority of children's workers in the church.* In Group's Children's Ministry online newsletter, Eugene C. Roehlkepartain, in his article "Olympic-Style Volunteer Training," proposes that 91 percent of children's ministry workers are women.[8]

Suppose a single mom desires a positive, mature male role model for her children. Where does she go? Likely, the natural father is not going to provide it. So she sends her children to school, but nearly everyone there is female. How about church? Shouldn't she be able to find some men who will take an interest in her kids and provide godly guidance to them? So she takes them to church, but 9 out of 10 of the workers there are women as well.

If a single mom wants her kids to experience influence from a godly, spiritually-minded man, and there is no one in her family like that, where does she go?

What does she do? There is little she *can* do by herself. As a result, we raise another generation of kids who have no firsthand knowledge of what it means to be a responsible man. The imbalance is dangerous.

The imbalance in the home has been put in the spotlight by sociologists and educators—even by our presidents. But little is being said about the imbalance in children's ministry. It's time that we not only took notice but took some steps to correct it.

In his article "Real Men Do Teach," my friend Gordon West presents this perspective:

> The absence of men in most children's ministries communicates a message we don't want to pass on. It's a hidden curriculum that subtly teaches children that Christianity is women's business. Little girls are subconsciously programmed to believe that few men are truly capable of being spiritual leaders. And little boys leave Sunday School subtly convinced that real men rarely get involved in church and are almost never excited about God.[9]

We need to *do* something about this.

To start, let's look at the Bible. I believe it gives us a clear picture of the validity of gender balance in children's ministry.

Mothering and Fathering in the Bible

The Activity of God

Genesis 1:27 says, *"So God created man in his own image, in the image of God he created him; male and female he created them."*

When asked, "How are we created in the image of God?" Bible schol-ars, pastors and teachers have been quick with their answers—"Oh, that refers to our soul and spirit." I thought that sounded logical. Obviously, I am not *physically* created in the image of God, because God doesn't have a body. So it's got to be my soul and spirit. "Moral nature," "tri-unity," "per-sonality," "God-consciousness"—these are also words that biblical author-ities mention as illustrating how we were made in His image.

However, it is significant that in context, the third phrase of Genesis 1:27 is the only detail given about how we were made in God's image. He, in making us in His image, created us *male* and *female*. As I said above, this cannot be in reference to our physical qualities of maleness and female-ness, because God doesn't have a body. It is the nonphysical qualities of masculinity and femininity that reflect God's image.

Think of it this way: If you really want to know what true masculinity is, where do you look? Do you look to some young, virile professional foot-ball player (Tim Tebow, for example)? No—you look to God and His char-acteristics. If you want to know what true femininity is, where do you look? Do you look to a supermodel? No—you look to God and His characteristics.

How do we see both masculinity and femininity as an aspect of God's image? Certainly not in sexuality or sensuality—that is the satanic distor-tion we see in so many other religions. They are not seen in position, either. God clearly fills the position of Father—which is why He is always called that in Scripture—and never of mother. Calling God "mother," which some religious groups do, is simply unbiblical.

So where do we see the masculinity and femininity of God played out? We see them realized in His *activity* toward us.

God Does Fathering Things

It is no surprise to you readers that God "fathers" us. We would expect no less, based on the hundreds of times God is referred to as "Father" in Scrip-ture. One clear example is in Proverbs 3:12, where the fathering activity of God is specifically mentioned: *"Because the LORD disciplines those he loves, as a father the son he delights in."* Notice the specific fathering activity mentioned here: *discipline*.

God Does Mothering Things

In addition, God "mothers" us. But we never once read of "Mother God" in Scripture—and the absence of that term must be a big caution to those who would make God feminine. However, God the Father does do moth-ering things. God says, as recorded in Isaiah 66:13: *"As a mother comforts her child, so will I comfort you; and you will be comforted over Jerusalem."* Notice the specific mothering activity mentioned here: *comfort.*

We can't overlook the mothering activity of God. In fact, the mothering activities of the God of the Bible differentiate Him from other god concepts. Allah, the god of Islam, is not perceived to be "mothering" at all. There are feminine gods in Hinduism, but they are seen to be either procreative or sensual. A god who "mothers" in the sense of loving comfort and nurture is foreign to all other concepts of God, making the God of the Bible unique.

The God of the Bible is unique from all other god-concepts in that our God is loving and nurturing. In other words, He is a *mothering* God.

Therefore, fathering and mothering are both characteristic activities of God. Fathering and mothering are also seen in Scripture as part of the spiritual training in the home.

Spiritual Training in the Home

In the most concise command in the New Testament concerning the spiritual training of children in the home, two concepts are used: *training* and *instruction.*

> *And, ye fathers, provoke not your children to wrath: but bring them up in the nurture and admonition of the Lord* (Eph. 6:4, *KJV*)

I appreciate the *KJV* translation of this verse because I believe it best catches the difference between the two Greek words that are translated here as "nurture" and "admonition." "Admonition" is the translation of the Greek word *paideia,* which is most often translated as "discipline" in Scripture. One example is found in Hebrews 12:7: *"God is treating you as sons. For what son is not disciplined by his father?"*

Paideia contains the idea of steering a boat: you get the boat where you want it to go by constantly correcting its course. It is stern direction (pun intended). Of course, both mothers and fathers can provide this kind of direction—but, generally speaking, it comes more naturally to a dad. Whether it is provided by a dad or by a mom when there is no dad present, this aspect of spiritual upbringing in the home is essential to a child's healthy spiritual growth.

The second term, *nouthesia*, is translated as "nurture" in the *KJV*. It also means to instruct, but it is gentler, indicating instructing more with words than correction. Most Bible versions simply translate this as "instruction," with a notable exception in the *KJV*, which, as we have seen, translates it as "nurture." In addition, the main verb of the sentence, *ektrepho*, means "nourish to maturity." Both of these have more of a nuance of mothering. As with discipline, the more tender approach can be provided by both mothers and fathers, but generally comes more naturally to a mom. It also is an essential element in the child's spiritual development.

We all get it: For the optimal spiritual development of children in the home, both fathering and mothering are critical! But fathering and mothering are also important in the church.

Discipleship in the Church

Discipleship in the setting of the local church also demands both a mothering and a fathering approach. We see this when the apostle Paul recounts his ministry among the Thessalonian believers. In 1 Thessalonians 2:7, Paul wrote that he, Silas and Timothy were *"gentle among you, like a mother caring for her little children."* The image is of a *nursing* mother caring for a very *little* child. The concept of mothering as a part of discipleship couldn't be clearer.

Then, just four verses later, he adds, *"For you know that we dealt with each of you as a father deals with his own children, encouraging, comforting and urging you to live lives worthy of God, who calls you into his kingdom and glory"* (vv. 11-12).

Is it any wonder that Paul used these two metaphors to describe his ministry to the church at Thessalonica? Young disciples—like young children—*need* a mothering approach. They *need* gentleness and nurture because, like a baby, they often are unable to feed themselves and care for themselves spiritually. Yet, young disciples also need urging and challenging and exhorting—the fathering approach. *Both* are critical to the discipleship process.

Summary

Before we go on to the implications for children's ministry, let me state what I believe . . .

- Fathering is different than mothering.
- Both fathering and mothering reflect the activity of God toward us.
- Both are needed for optimal child development in the home.
- Both are essential to the discipleship process.

Notes

1. Matt Daniels, cited in George Berkin, "Families with Fathers Fare best," NJ.com, June 18, 2010. http://blog.nj.com/njv_george_berkin/2010/06/families_with_fathers_fare_bes.html.
2. David Blankenhorn, *Fatherless America* (New York: Basic Books, 1995), p. 26.
3. Ibid., p. 30.
4. Ibid., p. 42.
5. Robbie Low is a vicar of St. Peter's, Bushey Heath, a parish of the Church of England. His full article can be found at http://touchstonemag.com/archives/article.php?id=16-05-024-v#ixzz1vp Sw5776.
6. "The Extent of Fatherlessness," Fathers.com. http://www.fathers.com/content/index.php?option=com_content&task=view&id=336.
7. U.S. Department of Labor, Bureau of Labor Statistics, "Current Population Survey: Table 11, Employed Persons by Detailed Occupation, Sex, Race, and Hispanic or Latino Ethnicity, 2007 Annual Averages." http://www.bls.gov/cps/cpsaat11.htm.
8. Eugene C. Roehlkepartain, "Olympic-Style Volunteer Training," *Children's Ministry*. http://childrensministry.com/articles/olympic-style-volunteer-training.
9. Gordon West, "Real Men Do Teach!" *Children's Ministry*. http://childrensministry.com/articles/real-men-do-teach!?p=2.

GENDER BALANCE IN CHILDREN'S MINISTRY

Why Balance Is Important

This section is not about merely balancing gender. If that were the case, this chapter would be insignificant and not worth reading. Instead, this is about bringing a balanced approach of mothering and fathering to the discipleship process that is critical to both boys and girls.

Is it better for children's ministry to be characterized by relatively balanced numbers between men and women? Absolutely. But in most churches (there are exceptions), reality is far from ideal.

This is not about merely balancing gender. If that were the case, this chapter would be insignificant and not worth reading.

When volunteers in children's ministry are primarily *women*, it makes sense that the approach may tend to be primarily mothering. When the volunteers are primarily *men*, it makes sense that the approach may be primarily fathering. If mothering comes more naturally to women and fathering to men, it also makes sense that we strive for a balance between men and women in children's ministry.

Larry Fowler

So what is the difference between fathering and mothering in discipleship? Sociologists tell us that mothers tend to emphasize the emotional security of their children, while fathers tend to stress competition and risk taking. Mothers also tend to seek the immediate wellbeing of the child, while fathers tend to foster long-term autonomy and independence. Children of both sexes appear to learn self-control and responsibility primarily from their fathers.

Therefore, a ministry that is primarily served by women will likely provide a caring, loving, safe environment but may not emphasize challenge, risk-taking and "Giving God all you've got."

I've seen the mothering approach often in children's ministry mission statements. Here is one: "To nurture a love of God and His Word in a caring and loving environment." It's wonderful! Who wouldn't want his or her child there? But it is a mothering-only statement. When I've taught about this subject, I've shown this particular mission statement to my students and then asked them to come up with one that is a "fathering" mission statement. I remember one group that managed to get both hunting and fishing into theirs. It was something like "We hunt down spiritual truths and fish for children who want to follow God." That was unique! But even if the "fathering" mission statements didn't include outdoor, male-dominated activities, they *all* were distinctively different from the mothering sample I gave them.

My students got the point: a mothering approach is essential in children's ministry—but so is fathering. Yet, the fathering approach it is often lacking.

So how do you get a better balance between mothering and fathering? Get the workers who will more naturally provide that balance. In other words, recruit more men. Then, give them the freedom to add their unique contribution to ministry. Remember, getting more men in children's ministry is *never* the end goal; it is the *means* to the end, which is to provide balanced, healthy discipleship for the children God gives you to shepherd. If I ever see that men have become the majority in children's ministry, then I'll write a chapter about how to recruit women. Until then, my appeal is to recruit more men.

How to Recruit and Retain Men

Success in recruiting men and then keeping them involved begins in how you think about the process. Here are five critical steps to get more men on board and, by so doing, bring gender balance to your children's ministry.

1. Think Vision

Gender balance in your ministry begins with what you communicate when you recruit—and then the vision you cast to those already involved. Men need *vision*. If your recruiting method is, "We need help in the second grade class," who is more likely to respond—men or women? Many conversations with children's ministry leaders have affirmed what I believe—women tend to be better "rescuers" than men. If your recruiting plea is "rescue us," you will most likely recruit women more than men. Most men, though they are willing to "help", respond better to a plea for workers that constantly emphasizes the cause and purpose of children's ministry.

Your effectiveness begins with the main messages you communicate about your ministry.

Your Key Statements

Therefore, balance your key statements about children's ministry. By key statements, I mean your vision and purpose statements—or any other term you give words and phrases that give direction to your workers. Start with analysis. Is your key statement . . .

- Primarily about *environment?* Here's a *mothering* environment statement: "Welcome to Children's Ministry (I will just use our generic term—you substitute what you call yours), where your child will feel safe and loved." Of *course* a safe, loving environment is critical. But don't forget, if you paint a picture of children's ministry that gives potential workers an image of pastels, peace and paradise, it may sound great to the nervous mom who is dropping off her kids, but it will do little to recruit men into your ministry. Men need an environment of energy, action and accomplishment. So let's transform that into an alternative *fathering* statement: "Welcome to Children's Ministry, where your child will feel challenged and empowered." While we don't want to leave out *safe* and *loved,* men are more likely to respond to this kind of a statement.

- Primarily about *content/curriculum?* Here's an inadequate version: "In Children's Ministry, your child will be taught God's Word." This particular statement is inadequate because the focus is teacher-centered rather than learning-centered. It also implies that if you work in children's ministry, you will be teaching—something that scares off many potential male volunteers.

- Primarily about *vision* and *outcome?* "In children's ministry, your child will make significant steps toward becoming a lifelong Christ-follower." This one is really lofty, and we know it likely won't happen with every child we minister to. So we tend to avoid statements like this. But this is the kind of a statement that will appeal more to men. Read the U.S. Marines statement in the call-out. Analyze it and think, *How would this statement be so attractive to young men?*

**On the United States Marines home page:
"We will make Marines. We will win our Nation's battles.
We will develop quality citizens."**

Your Informal Vocabulary

Beyond the key statements, check the language you use in informal conversations, newsletters, and when talking to groups of potential workers. Begin to recognize the key contributions of both men and women in your ministry. Think about what you might say that would appeal more to men.

Close your eyes, and let your imagination put an image with this phrase: "children's teachers." Did your image include both genders, or did you only see women? If so, check how that comes out in your speech. It may be that you use "she" too much when referring to a children's worker.

Start transparent conversations with men in your church who know something of your children's ministry. Ask them, "Do you think that working in children's ministry in our church is attractive to men? Why, or why not?" If they answer in the negative, then your children's ministry leaders must begin by changing that impression.

Your Deliberate Vision-casting to Men

While your overall vision statement may need to be adjusted to include the contributions of men, you must also be prepared to help men see their unique contribution: In other words, you want to communicate to them, "No woman can do what you can do . . ."

In the fall of 2010, I had the privilege of having breakfast with Dr. Ken Canfield. Dr. Canfield has distinguished himself with a lifetime devoted to parenting and fathering. He is the founder of the National Center for Fathering, and has written numerous books, including the award-winning *The 7 Secrets of Effective Fathers*.[1] He said something that struck me as quite insightful (he says a lot of insightful things). His comment was something like this: "You know, Larry, I've stopped talking about parenting. Instead, I've started talking about fathering and mothering, because when I talk about parenting, the husband is sitting in the audience beside his wife thinking, *That's a great idea—my wife will be really good at that*. And I want dads to see their unique responsibility and their unique contribution to raising their children."

The same is true in children's ministry. Unless we begin persuading men that they—as men—have something unique to contribute to the spiritual development of children, most of them "will let the women do it."

2. Think Mount Whitney

At a height of 14,497 feet, Mount Whitney, in northern California, is the tallest mountain peak in the contiguous United States. For mountain climbers, conquering the ascent is quite a challenge and is worth celebrating when it is accomplished. My mountain-climbing list of accomplishments is a short one. I've only climbed Blodgett Peak near Colorado Springs—a short 2,500-foot climb from the base to the peak. The guys in our family did it together, and while it was a fairly easy climb, I was still pretty stoked because we conquered it.

Whether they are mountain climbers or not, men need a challenge. They will respond best when the challenge is clear. The more monumental the task is, the greater the appeal to pursue it. That doesn't mean they will jump in just because you throw a challenge in front of them, as they also need to have a pretty good idea that they can succeed. Think of your message to recruit men this way:

Low-threat entry point   Big challenge

If you diminish the challenge, you will have a lower degree of success in recruiting men. At the same time, if you make the entry point too difficult, they will be less likely to come on board. (We will talk more about the entry point later in the chapter.) Here's a sample "recruiting pitch" that includes these first two points:

Jason, you know we are all about making significant changes in the lives of the kids God has entrusted to us in children's ministry. We believe that God has given us a small window of time to impact them for the rest of their lives, and we want to do everything we can to take advantage of that window. I can't imagine a ministry anywhere that can have a more monumental impact for God in the lives of others than what He has given us to do. And we are constantly looking for people to join us in our mission. That's why I wanted to talk to you. I believe you could be an important part of our team. I think you can challenge these kids and be an example to them. I know that children's ministry is new to you, so here's what I'd like to propose: we have a group of 6 to 7 children with whom there is already a veteran worker serving. Would you be willing to sit in with that person for the next month and simply love the kids in the group and show interest in their lives? That will give you a feel for what we do, and then we can talk about you becoming more involved in the days ahead.

Did you pick up on the "big challenge" and the "low-threat entry point?" Did you identify the "vision statements?" These are essential in engaging men in children's ministry who are first-timers.

Men need a challenge. They are highly motivated by goals and/or competition. "Defeat the enemy" is a recruiting/retention cry that works with men. The enemy can be the world, the flesh or the devil, or something else biblical. Men want to *win*. It is up to you to position your children's ministry so that they believe they are joining a winning effort in battling the enemy.

Can I suggest an exercise? Visit an Armed Services website yourself. Notice how many of the images and expressions are those of challenge and adventure. While we know that many young women are also recruited, I am certain you will pick up on how and why it is so appealing to young men. You will learn a lot!

3. Think Easy Chair

Many men have a chair in their house that is "theirs." I do, and I like it a lot. It's a recliner, and it is *so* comfortable. Have you ever noticed where men congregate in homes that have both a formal living room and a family room? It's not the formal living room; it is the family room—where the recliner is—or wherever they feel more *comfortable*.

Helping men feel comfortable is also critical in children's ministry. We can do a lot to modify the environment of children's ministry so that involvement feels more natural. It may be helpful to ask, "What might drive a man away?" Or maybe a better question is, "What might keep a man from coming in?"

Here are some possibilities.

The Décor
Most children's ministry areas are decorated with the children in mind, so this is not so much of an issue. However, it can be: If there are lots of pastels and butterflies and flowers—you get the picture—it won't be so welcoming to men—OR boys!

Did you look at the U.S. Marines website? Did you see the design elements that might attract young men? Think through your children's ministry wing. Is it balanced in its appeal, or could it use some redecorating?

The Policies
Cassandra[2] was sharing enthusiastically about her church's child protection policies in our discussion group. "We are so careful, that we don't even let men change diapers." The ladies in the group were impressed as Cassandra went on to share about how diligent her church was in following through on CP procedures. But I was bothered. Why? Because I have discovered that such policies leave men feeling distrusted and accused before they ever start. Her comment has motivated me to regularly ask men, "What child protection policies may have the unintended effect of driving good men away from children's ministry?" Here are a couple of the big ones:

- *Changing babies' diapers.* Some child protection policies actually prohibit this for men. When I discuss this with men, nearly every time the response I get back is, "It's not that I *want* to change diapers—I just don't want to be told that I can't."

- *Going in the bathroom.* Many men say, "I'm not clear about the rule— if a little boy comes in while I am in there, do I have to go out? Do I tell him 'stay out' until I go out? Do I have to find another man who will go into the bathroom with me?" (Ladies do this all the time with one another, but it feels really weird to men.)

Some churches have even adopted a policy that no men are allowed in the preschool departments at all—even posting signs to that effect. I understand their motivation—to keep the predator at bay—but it is ironic to me that they have such a policy and yet they allow men to work with the children in all the other age levels, when the risk is greater. I wonder how they are doing in recruiting men . . .

In our eagerness to prevent the predator from having access to children in our children's ministry (a good thing—no, an *essential* thing), have we swung the pendulum so far that we also deter men in general from participating? Is prevention possible without making men run the other direction? It is worth asking the question.

Think through the "easy chair" analogy—decide what can help a man feel more comfortable in your children's ministry, and then take action!

4. Think Play Guns

If you take some boys on a walk, it isn't very long until one or two of them have picked up a stick. And what does the stick become? A sword or a gun. Before you know it there will be a pretend battle going on. Little boys will turn just about any object into a weapon and any activity into a competition. It is important to remember that many of the men in our churches have not lost that tendency!

For a minute, think of your own personal answer to this question:

What is your very best memory of your father?

Some of us are fortunate to have many "best memories." For others, it may be hard to think of even one. But as I have asked this question to audiences, the answers I get back almost always fall into one category: an *activity*. Why is that so true? Because our dads were likely more at ease, more comfortable, more enthusiastic, more *themselves*, when doing an activity. Men usually communicate better while doing an activity.

If you want to recruit more men, you must create *activity* entry positions for them to fill.

So, if you want to recruit more men, you must create *activity* entry positions for them to fill, and you might need to make competition a part of it. By an activity entry point, I mean something more physical—something they can *do*. In Awana, we have various roles spelled out in our clubs: directors, leaders, and so on. All are filled by a majority of women (our numbers are 73 percent women—better than the national norm, but not close to satisfactory), but men fill one position at a rate of 56 percent. Can you guess which one it is? Drum roll, please . . . *game director!* Is that surprising? Or is it a statistic that can educate us concerning Sunday ministries as well?

You may need to create some new positions. They may have to do with technology, events, security or activities, but you can't expect to effectively increase the number of men in your ministry without them. Then make sure your positions are *entry* positions—in other words, only move those men into roles that have greater spiritual responsibility as they get comfortable.

5. Think Rugby

I have never played rugby, but I greatly admire those who do. It's my opinion that rugby is the "man's man" sport. Of course, it is hugely competitive, and there is a goal, with a winner and a loser. But there are several elements that make rugby unique; it is *rough*—like football, but without pads—and there is a huge risk of injury.

That image of rugby is helpful in describing ministry that is attractive to men.

Men Need to Serve Shoulder-to-Shoulder

Rugby is played shoulder-to-shoulder—the players line up in a single line across the field, side by side. You've likely heard it said that women's ministry happens face-to-face and men's ministry happens shoulder-to-shoulder. In other words, it mirrors rugby. It is not only true for ministering *to* men, but I also believe it is true for getting men to minister. Shoulder-to-shoulder means that, together, they are tackling an activity like a rugby team runs down the field.

Think what your ministry would look like if you adopted the same approach. Ask the question, "Are the ministry positions I need filled more face-to-face or shoulder-to-shoulder?" Face-to-face positions mean that you are alone—and relational—and vulnerable—all of which aren't too appealing to most men. Two positions that are usually face-to-face positions are teacher and small group leader (when by yourself).

Men Need Other Men

Rugby is a true *team sport*. One player may handle the ball and run with it as far as he can before he is tackled, but as he is going down, the other players have his back—they are right behind him where they can get the ball from him and then run. We need to make sure that men aren't isolated in their service. Here is what I mean: What would happen if you tried to recruit men to an otherwise all-woman classroom? I've heard the stories;

a man volunteers to help with the four-year-olds, but when he gets there, every other worker is a woman. What do you think the likelihood is that a man will stay engaged for very long in that situation? On the other hand, let men compete together or work together or struggle together—and their commitment level will skyrocket.

Men Need a Chance to Win

Men *love* to compete—and of course that is part of the attraction of sports. In his book, *Why Men Hate Going to Church*, David Murrow wrote, "If you want to capture the heart of a man—especially a younger man—you have to offer him a shot at greatness. Men will not invest themselves whole-heartedly in any endeavor that does not offer this possibility.[3] What does Murrow mean? That triumph over obstacles and opposition, achievement of goals or winning a competition are all paths to feeling great in some way. Can a man do those things in your children's ministry? What does triumph, achievement or winning look like in what you do? If you can't define them or you don't, you will be less effective in getting men involved.

Fulfill the Vision

You can do it. You can balance genders in your children's ministry—but you must be strategic in recruiting and attracting men. Single moms who want godly masculine influences in their children's lives will thank you. The kids will thank you. And the men will thank you as well.

Notes
1. Ken R. Canfield, *The 7 Secrets of Effective Fathers* (Carol Stream, IL: Tyndale, 2002).
2. Not her real name.
3. David Murrow, *Why Men Hate Going to Church* (Thomas Nelson, Nashville, TN, 2005), p. 99.

THANK GOD FOR MEN—AND WOMEN!

Take a minute to feel grateful.

Here is my minute: When our children were young, Paul worked in our church with early elementary kids. He was a silver-haired, sophisticated gentleman and a great example of godliness to all of them. He was often the only man serving with that age group, but that didn't faze him, because he saw it as his ministry. He never wanted to teach, but he knew he could have an impact just by being there—and loving children. Our own two kids loved him back, and he had a significant, positive impact on them. *Thank you, Paul Nedeleff.*

Who is providing a godly example of masculinity—or femininity—to the children in your life? Take a moment to rejoice over his or her positive influence—and then go tell that person how much you appreciate what he or she is doing.

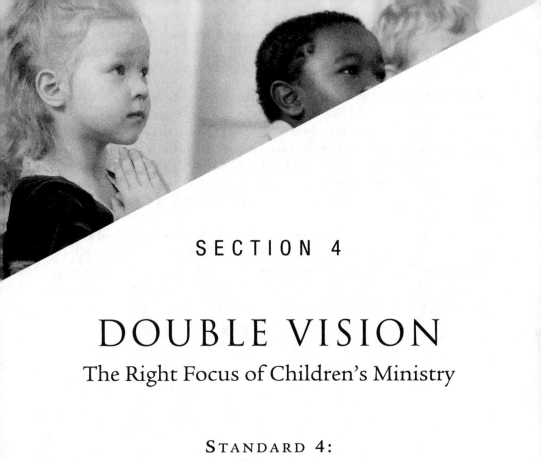

SECTION 4

DOUBLE VISION
The Right Focus of Children's Ministry

S TANDARD 4:
We are locked on to the needs of children and
the desired spiritual outcome in their lives.

You see the trouble we are in: Jerusalem lies in ruins,
and its gates have been burned with fire. Come, let us rebuild the
wall of Jerusalem, and we will no longer be a disgrace.
N EHEMIAH 2:17

I take for granted that I have two eyes that work. However, I can easily experiment with what it is like to not have both eyes functioning correctly; all I have to do is shut one and then try to walk down a hallway or up some steps and even the most normal exercise becomes a bit of a challenge.

Vision problems can severely inhibit our ability to function—whether we are talking about our physical eyesight or our figurative "vision"—and that is the subject of this next section. In it, I want you to think about *double vision*.

Double vision (in reference to its physical, medical meaning) is a bad thing, but I am asking you to think of it as a good thing when it applies to ministry. Here's what I mean: When we work with children, we must keep two things in clear view all the time—in that way, we must have *double vision*. I will describe what we must keep clear in the following pages.

THE TWO LENSES OF CHILDREN'S MINISTRY

How to Focus Binoculars

Have you ever looked through binoculars? What you should see when you look through them is a round circle (called the field of view) surrounded by blackness. One or both of the lenses may be out of focus when you first look through them, and as a result, there may be two blurry fields of view. So, you close one eye, and using the focus control, correct it. Then you repeat with the other lens. Once both lenses are individually focused, you use the central control to align both into one field of view.

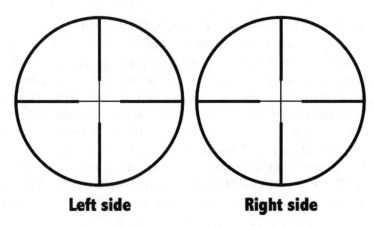

Left side   **Right side**

Larry Fowler

Binoculars are preferable over monoculars (only one lens) to see most things because of the added depth perception that comes from using both eyes and both lenses. But both lenses have to be focused in order to work.

Think of looking at your ministry through spiritual binoculars—two lenses, both of which have to be focused and then merged into one field of view. That is what we are going to do here: We are going to focus first on one ministry lens, then the other—and then align them together into one spiritual field of view. How do we focus them? By looking at Scripture, of course.

Lens One: Need

The Beauty and the Beggar

I am amazed by the focus of Peter and John told in Acts 3. The story begins this way:

> *One day Peter and John were going up to the temple at the time of prayer— at three in the afternoon* (v. 1).

It was the middle of the afternoon. There were still a lot of visitors in Jerusalem, so the crowd flowing into the temple was extra heavy. Peter and John, still in wonder of the reality of Jesus' resurrection appearances, joined the crowd that day.

> *Now a man crippled from birth was being carried to the temple gate called Beautiful, where he was put every day to beg from those going into the temple courts* (v. 2).

I've wondered why the temple gate was called Beautiful. My good friend Jerry Thorpe[1] says it was because it was . . . well . . . *beautiful*. In fact, people would stop and comment, "What a beautiful gate!" Maybe it was the color that made it so spectacular to the eyes, or maybe it was the architecture or the ornate design, or maybe it was all three. But in any case, it amazed people. Maybe it was new, fresh and clean—and that was why visitors from afar would come just to see the gate. As they came near it, everyone's eyes would have focused upward on the Beautiful Gate as they entered.

Beside the gate was the beggar. He was, in appearance, the antithesis of the gate. There was no beautiful color to his clothing, which was probably so old and filthy one could describe it as shades of dirt. And there was

Larry Fowler

no beautiful design to them—just the most plain of rags or material, probably torn and worn in addition to being dirty. And his "architecture"—his body—was crippled. His misshapen legs were hideous, sprawled in awkward directions. They were something you looked away from, not toward. Instead of exclaiming aloud, "How beautiful!" you muttered quietly to your companion, "How awful!"

For probably 20 years, at least, this man had been carried to the temple gate to beg.[2] Day after long day, and month after long month, and year after long year he sat there and said the same words. He didn't pay attention to faces any more, because if he looked too directly or too long, they would just look away. But somehow he felt prompted to directly ask Peter and John for help . . .

When he saw Peter and John about to enter, he asked them for money (v. 3).

It's likely that, just as we do today with the homeless, those walking by would be silently saying, *I hope he won't accost me.* Most of the time, the eyes of those entering the Beautiful Gate would have avoided looking at him completely, pretending not to notice. Probably, people were actually *glad* for the beauty of the gate so they didn't have to look at the beggar. But something highly unusual happened.

Peter looked straight at him, as did John. Then Peter said, "Look at us!" (v. 4).

Nobody said that to a beggar! Nobody actually *tried* to get the attention of a beggar. That was something a regular person avoided. It was so unusual that the beggar looked up, and his and Peter's gazes locked. Then, with a few words from Peter, and the power of the Holy Spirit, the crippled beggar's life was forever changed:

So the man gave them his attention, expecting to get something from them. Then Peter said, "Silver or gold I do not have, but what I have I give you. In the name of Jesus Christ of Nazareth, walk." Taking him by the right hand, he helped him up, and instantly the man's feet and ankles became strong. He jumped to his feet and began to walk. Then he went with them into the temple courts, walking and jumping, and praising God (vv. 5-8).

Think about where Peter and John looked. Everyone else in the crowd going into the temple *gazed at the environment* and *never saw the beggar.* Peter and John saw the beggar, and probably never noticed the Beautiful

Gate. They also saw beyond the surface need. Everyone else saw the beggar asking for money, but Peter saw the deeper need—healing—and believed God could provide it.

This is a potent and sobering reminder to us in children's ministry to do the same—to see the need of the beggar. Now let's look at the other lens.

Lens Two: Outcome

Shambles or Shame

Let me ask you a Bible trivia question, and you think of the answer before you read on. In the Old Testament book of Nehemiah, we learn of Nehemiah's journey to Jerusalem. He was likely born in exile and left Susa, the palace in the capital of Persia, to travel there.

Here's the question: *Why did he go?*

Not fair looking down further to see the answer!

If you answered, "To rebuild the broken-down wall," you are just like nearly everyone else to whom I've asked the question—wwrrooong! Think with me: chapter 1 of Nehemiah opens with him hearing of the conditions in Jerusalem, and it so moves him that he mourns and fasts for days. *For days!* Does it make sense that a bunch of out-of-place stones would be a reason to mourn? And fast? For *days* (see Neh. 1:4)? No, there's got to be more . . .

In chapter 2, Nehemiah is serving before the king in his role as cupbearer. That meant, of course, that his job—one that was given to only the most trusted servant—was to taste the palace food and drink before the king to make sure it had not been poisoned. Nehemiah's face looks so sad that the king takes notice of it. I'm sure that Nehemiah was doing all that he could to look healthy, because looking sick could cause quite a stir in the king's court. But he couldn't keep from it, and the king notices and asks, *"Why does your face look so sad when you are not ill? This can be nothing but sadness of heart"* (Neh. 2:2). Let me ask again—with so much at stake, does it make sense that a bunch of out-of-place stones would be the reason for such a downcast face? No, no—there's got to be more . . .

A few verses later, we learn what it is:

> Then I said to them, *"You see the trouble we are in: Jerusalem lies in ruins, and its gates have been burned with fire. Come, let us rebuild the wall of Jerusalem, and we will no longer be in disgrace"* (v. 17).

Aha! What caused Nehemiah to mourn and fast for days—and for his face to look so sad—was not the *ruins*, but the *disgrace*. He was not concerned so much with the physical condition of the wall, but with the spiritual outcome—that the reputation of Jerusalem (and therefore, the reputation of the God of Jerusalem) was shamed.

We don't understand this today, because our cities don't have walls. But in Nehemiah's day, the wall of a city was a source of pride—no respectable city would be without one. But the people who lived in Jerusalem had been daily walking over and around and in sight of the broken stones, and no one was doing anything to fix it! Jerusalem, the city of God, was a disgrace!

So why did Nehemiah go to Jerusalem? Not to rebuild the wall, but to remove the shame. Rebuilding the wall, however, was *how* he removed the disgrace. Notice his "success report" in Nehemiah 6:15-16 confirms this:

Report of the activity completed:	*So the wall was completed on the twenty-fifth of Elul, in fifty-two days* (v. 15).
Report of the political victory:	*When all our enemies heard about this, all the surrounding nations were afraid and lost their self-confidence* (v. 16a).
Report of the spiritual outcome:	*They realized that this work had been done with the help of our God* (v. 16b).

Identifying Spiritual Outcomes

Let's bring this principle home: Suppose someone is visiting your church and another church leader is showing him around. They come into your children's ministry program and watch for a minute or two. Then the visitor turns to you and asks, "What are you doing here?"

What is your answer? (Cooperate with me, please—think of your answer before you read on)

- Did you tell the visitor about the *program activity* that is going on? "Well, we are finishing up table time, which will end in a few minutes—then the kids will all go into the next room for our large group lesson." That's accurate, but it's not the best focus to lock on. Focus failure!

- Did you describe the *workers' activity*? "We are in a relationship-building time right now, and then we will take them into the next room where they will be taught a lesson." That's so important—

but it doesn't force examination of outcomes. My assessment: focus failure again!

- Did you describe the *curriculum content?* "The kids are learning the themes of the books of Old Testament history and how each relates to the story of redemption." That's so good—but it is shortsighted. My assessment: focus failure the third time!

- Did you describe the *spiritual activity?* "We are discipling these kids in their spiritual walk?" Really good—but it still only describes the present activity. Focus failure number four!

- Or did you describe the *spiritual outcome?* "We are taking one step today toward each of these children becoming lifelong followers of Jesus Christ."

Go back to Nehemiah 2:17 and notice the progression of Nehemiah's statement:

1. He pointed out the present condition: *"You see the trouble we are in?"*
2. He provided the supporting facts: *"Jerusalem lies in ruins, and its gates have been burned."*
3. He proposed a physical action: *"Come, let us rebuild the wall of Jerusalem."*
4. He projected a spiritual outcome: *"So that we will no longer be in disgrace."*

Present condition:	"These children are just beginning to form their life patterns and their worldview."
The supporting facts:	"They are at the stage of life where they have the greatest capacity for learning."
The physical action:	"So we are helping them master the big story of the Bible."
The spiritual outcome:	"So that they will have strong foundations of truth that will help them live for God all their lives."

Now let's apply that progression to children's ministry. Suppose you follow the same pattern with the visitor, and you respond to him with the words on the right side of the table:

Do you see? The *other* side of "double vision" is to have a clear focus of the desired spiritual outcome. Somebody needs to lock on to this focus—and that somebody needs to be you. *Your* focus in children's ministry must go further than simply the need or the activity; it needs to lock in on the spiritual outcome.

These two things must become your "double vision"—your two ministry focuses: the needs of the children and the desired spiritual outcome. Our model for this section looks like this: When we see them both clearly and they merge together for us into one field of view, we will have the right focus in our ministry.

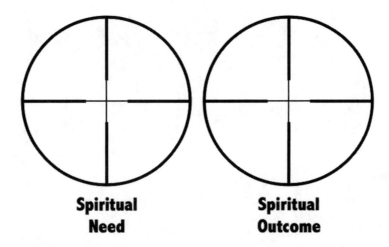

Spiritual Need **Spiritual Outcome**

In the next chapter, we will look at how to see with this double vision.

Notes

1. Jerry is a retired pastor and master of preaching, if there ever was one. He served for 36 years in Temple Baptist Church in Odessa, Texas, where God blessed his ministry with incredible growth and stability.
2. According to Acts 4:22, this man was more than 40 years old.

HOW TO GET YOUR MINISTRY IN FOCUS

Introduction

Our daughter Andrea was born at 4:05 AM on Sunday, July 18, 1976. I'm well aware that she was the star of the event, that Diane was the main player and hero, and that the doctor and nurses helped—but humor me for a little while and let me tell you what went on with *me*.

At the time, we were living in Riverside, California, where I was a young youth pastor. We had shared our anticipation with the youth group, and they were anxious along with us for the birth of the baby.

When the baby came, Diane had been in labor for about 12 hours—through the night—and I was by her side the whole time, trying to encourage and help her breathe. I didn't get any sleep at all. After the birth, I was *so* excited to see and hold my beautiful baby girl that adrenaline kept me going. In fact, several hours later—when baby Andrea went to sleep and Diane needed to—I decided to go to the church (since it was Sunday) and teach my youth group. I confess it wasn't that my devotion to my students was that high; I was just so anxious to tell them the news myself! Needless to say, I enjoyed sharing about Andrea's birth with everyone I could.

I went back to the hospital for the afternoon, and I remember watching the Olympics on the TV in Diane's room to stay awake. She slept some, but I was still operating on excitement. But by suppertime, adrenaline began to wane and loss of sleep began to take over, and I knew I had to go home and rest.

I drove home to our small house. The master bedroom was so tiny. It had only our bed and a nightstand in it, and they fit in the room only because the bed was in a corner against a wall.

I went straight to bed and fell fast asleep from exhaustion. Usually, I slept facing the edge of the bed, but that evening I was so tired that I fell asleep facing the wall. Some time in the evening, I roused just enough to become aware that there was a ringing noise. I was so out of it at first that I didn't know it was the phone. It seemed so *loud,* and I was so *tired*, I just wanted to get it to *stop!* (Of course the ringing was coming from the wall phone, which was not in the bedroom but in the hallway down by the kitchen.)

I got out of bed to try to find the phone (somehow I sensed that was what it was). My thoughts were too fuzzy to remember to turn on the light on the nightstand, and I just started moving. Unfortunately, I starting moving in the wrong direction—*away* from edge of the bed—and cracked my head into the wall. That about knocked me silly. Now I was *really* out of it. I couldn't figure out why the wall was there. Where was I? I wanted to turn that annoying ringing off, but I just couldn't get my bearings. After about three or four attempts, I found an edge to the bed and crawled off, still not able to focus clearly. Then I found what I thought was the hallway door, opened it and walked straight ahead—until I walked into some clothes on hangers. Now where was I? Oh . . . in the closet. I stumbled in the dark to the hallway, but wouldn't you know the phone stopped ringing as soon as I got there.

A few minutes later it rang again, and it was one of the youth group guys calling to congratulate me. He had no clue of the difficulty I'd had just to pick up the phone.

*   *   *   *   *

Being that disoriented was the strangest feeling I hope to never feel again. But I've felt almost that unfocused in my ministry at times. I've asked, "So—what *should* I be doing?" and not had a clue. I've also asked, "Am I doing the right thing?" or "Am I going in the right direction?"

How about you? Have you ever felt like that in ministry? Have you ever felt unsure of which direction to go? Have you felt out of focus? Unclear? In the dark?

Let's begin the process of getting back to a clear focus.

Children's Needs in Clear Focus

The first "lens" of children's ministry, practically stated, is this: *You have to know the needs of the children you work with.*

Do you? Say, for example, you have a small group. How readily could you fill out this chart for each child?

Name of Child	Universal Need(s)	Biggest Spiritual Need(s)	Biggest Felt Need(s)

Can you even fill it in? Or do you have to admit, "I don't know"? If you can fill it in, you will begin to have direction for what you need to do as a minister to children.

Maybe you'd like some help to get started. Here are some things you could put in the second column, under "universal needs:"

- to be loved
- to be safe
- to be valued

Those are true needs of every child in the world, aren't they?

Then assess their spiritual needs. Is each child a professing believer? Where are they in their biblical knowledge? In their attitude toward spiritual things? Are they obedient toward God? The list could be very long, but could you put at least two spiritual needs by each child's name?

Finally, there are felt needs. If we asked the children, "What do you need?" and they understood what we meant, would some say "comfort" or "a happy home" or "a friend?" In other words, what are the needs they consciously feel? Can you put one or two of these needs by each child's name?

Maybe you laughed when you saw the chart, because you thought, *There's only five lines—I've got 45 in my group!* If that is your ratio, then you will never know their needs unless you find a way—or the volunteers who work with you find a way—to get to know them individually (more about that in section 5). You know, I really empathize with those of you who serve large groups of children. You have a challenge, don't you? In fact, the larger the group, the greater the challenge to identify *individual* needs. That doesn't change the fact that the better we identify the needs, the better direction we will have in ministry.

Then keep your focus riveted on those needs. It is so easy to get distracted. Let's return to Scripture to illustrate two cautions. Here is the first one.

Don't Get Distracted by the Beautiful Gate

We can get so focused on our Beautiful Gate that we also fail to notice the beggar. What is our beautiful gate? Anything that distracts us from seeing needs. Maybe it *is* something beautiful, like décor, or maybe it is technology or media or organization or . . . But it is *our* distraction.

Who are the beggars? Every child. Every child needs our attention, our love. In a spiritual sense, that beggar in the story represents every one of them.

Was there anything bad or evil with the Beautiful Gate? Of course not. It was probably decorated to honor God. After all, it was the entrance to the temple. However, most people who entered it were looking at it instead of the beggar . . . *they were looking at the wrong thing.*

The last couple of decades have provided a lot of emphasis upon carefully designed and decorated children's ministry areas in churches. As I stated before, it's not just the physical décor; our time and energy can be consumed with technology and other elements of our environment. And not only do we enjoy *seeing* it, but we also put lots of time and money into *creating* it.

What is your Beautiful Gate? Is it technology or media? I confess that while I am far from savvy with using media, I have too often spent hours trying to perfect a video insert into my lesson, and then I end up not having time to really make sure that the biblical truth I am presenting is going to connect with the hearts of the kids. In other words, I craft my lesson to be beautiful, and in doing so, I neglect to make sure it meets the needs of a beggar.

Here's a second caution.

Don't Get Focused Merely on *Numbers*

Annette, one of my children's ministry friends, complained, "I am getting so much pressure from my senior pastor to grow. It seems like all he cares about is numbers."

I empathized with Annette. But I also suspect that her senior pastor would say, "Annette, numbers represent souls. And we are in ministry to reach as many of those as we can."

This tension around growth and numbers has caused me to ask the WWJD question—or more accurately, the WDJD question: "What DID Jesus do?"

I have some observations about Jesus and "numbers."

- *Never once did Jesus mention numbers.* The only reference to the size of crowds is made by the writers of the Gospels, but never by Jesus.

- *Never once did Jesus indicate His pleasure over the size of the crowd.* There is simply no record of Him ever saying anything remotely like, "I'm really excited to see how many of you came out today."

- *Large crowds actually seemed to wear Jesus out.* The Gospels tell us He wanted to get *away* from the crowds—but on the other hand, He was never so worn out that He refused to minister to an individual.

- *At the same time, Jesus challenged His disciples with the largest numbers of all:* He said, "Go into all the world," "teach all nations," and preach the gospel to "every person" (see Matt. 28:19-20).

Here's my conclusion: While Jesus had a *global vision*, He never had a *numbers focus*. His focus was always locked on the individual and his or her need. Remember Matthew 9:36?

When he saw the crowds, he had compassion on them, because they were harassed and helpless, like sheep without a shepherd.

What was Jesus' internal reaction to large numbers of people coming to follow Him? Was He quietly pleased? Satisfied that His message was being heard by so many? No. Jesus' internal response was one of being burdened by their need. An examination of the Gospel accounts will reveal that was *always* His focus.

While Jesus had a global vision, *He never had a numbers focus.*

Wouldn't we improve our ministries if we could emulate Him better in this way? If we focused on needs instead of numbers? Let me summarize what I want you to learn:

To best determine the direction of your ministry,
you must clearly focus on the needs of the children you are ministering to.

The Long-term Outcome in Clear Focus

How far into the future do you look?

I was once asked a great question in a group setting: "Larry, if you could change one thing in children's ministry, what would it be?" I said, "I would stop the emphasis on practical application." My questioner looked stunned. I went on to explain there's nothing wrong with practical application, except that it doesn't look out far enough and we may miss some very important approaches if we allow it to rule. Whether or not the children apply the lesson one week or not is not as critical as a longer vision. It may very well be a vital step toward our desirable outcome, but it is only one step—and it is usually a behavioral one. Molding the heart toward a more permanent outcome is what we must keep in focus.

Will you look to a more distant outcome? There has been so much made of the research in recent years that our Christian young people, upon becoming young adults, are abandoning the church. Keeping that factor in mind and determining to change the statistics gives us a much better vision than just saying, "What do we want the outcome to be this week—or this month?"

In my book *Raising a Modern-Day Joseph*, I relate an airplane conversation I had with a young dad.[1] As part of the conversation, I asked him this question: "What do you want to be able to say about your children when they are 30?" This father of two toddlers, though he was a strategist at work, confessed that he had never thought about that question. I regularly ask the same question of parents when I have teaching opportunities. I imagine that you are not surprised at my findings, as most parents have *never* even discussed the topic at all.

The same kind of distant vista should be in our field of view in children's ministry. We should be asking, "What do we want to be able to say about these children when they are 30?" I know you can answer that question quickly: We want to see the children in our ministry become lifelong, deeply devoted followers of Christ.

Keeping that outcome clearly in view, though, prompts questions— good questions: "If that is our goal, what do children need to learn and experience and master when they are five years old? Eight years old? Twelve years old? Sequential learning and sequential steps toward maturity become our guide in curriculum decisions.

One Sunday after church, Diane and I wanted to drop off a letter at a post office. There was one on the other side of our church a few miles, in a neighborhood we usually did not travel through. After dropping off the letter, we started home, and feeling adventurous, I turned on a street that was new to us. "Let's see if we can get home on this one." I was up for exploring. But it only took us deep into a housing tract. I tried to figure out where to go, but I had to turn around more than a few times in dead-end streets or cul-de-sacs and, wouldn't you know it, we ended up back where we started. I learned my lesson and stuck to streets familiar to me. What was the problem? Not the sense of adventure, but rather that I didn't check a map or a GPS to see if my route would take me where I wanted to go.

Do you ever do that in your ministry? Do you ever choose curriculum, start a project or implement a program with the thought *let's try this*? And yet, you haven't really examined whether it can get you to the spiritual outcome you desire?

When we do have that spiritual outcome in focus, we will work from the long-term down to the short-term. It will impact our planning, our curriculum choices, our projects and our programs.

- We will no longer ask, "What shall we teach this week or this quarter?" before we have the answer to "What should the children learn this year?"
- We will not merely coexist with the youth ministry but will cooperate with them and coordinate curriculum and strategies together.
- We will be strategic in giving children opportunities to serve and exercise their faith.
- We will involve parents in the spiritual discipleship process.

This realization has dramatically affected our curriculum design in Awana. We now talk constantly about thinking in terms of ages 2 to 18 (the ages of childhood). We never ask, "What shall we develop for this year?" because all of our planning of what we will teach, and when, is with the whole 16-year span in mind.

Let me encourage you to ask the question about your children that I asked the young dad on the plane. The question relates to both the children in your home and in your ministry. When you have a clear answer, you will have better direction.

Back to Binoculars

Remember how, with binoculars, you focus one lens and then the other, and then you bring the images together? Now do the same with what we have discussed. You will have the direction of where to go and what to do when you bring these three ideas together:

1. You have a clear focus locked on to the spiritual needs of your children.
2. You also have a clear focus locked on to the spiritual outcome.
3. You see them converge into one clear picture.

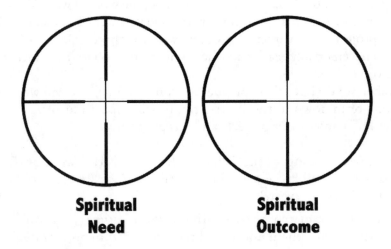

**Spiritual
Need**

**Spiritual
Outcome**

In Focus and Locked On

At the beginning of the first Gulf War, dubbed Desert Storm, Americans first became familiar with laser-guided smart bombs. I remember marveling during some of the first press conferences broadcast on CNN: General Norman Schwarzkopf presided, showing America a video of the action. "Stormin' Norman" first showed us the satellite image of a building where Iraqi munitions were stored. Next was a clip of our fighter jets flying toward the target. Then we saw the release of a smart bomb—locked on to a laser signal—precisely *pierce the door* of an Iraqi ammunitions storage building. The accuracy was astounding.

I felt such pride in our military—that we could neutralize the enemy's weapons and at the same time minimize the danger of killing civilians. Though I was no expert in military tactics (I'm still not), I got it: the ability to lock on the target and hit it so accurately was a game changer in the war and in our military future.

Imagine the effectiveness of our fighter jets if the pilot relaxed and let the laser that guided the bomb wander. Locking on to a target—the right target—in ministry is vital as well. Lose the target out of our sights, and instead of accomplishing our mission, we can also cause collateral damage. I call it "focus failure."

In the normal routine things you do to minister to kids, do your sights stay locked on the target?

I have a lot of confidence that you are already convinced that the outcome we need to lock on to is a lifelong devoted follower of Jesus Christ. But from week to week in ministry, in the routine things we do, I have a concern: Do we *stay* locked on to it, or do we get distracted?

Focus Failure

I have observed far too many instances of focus failure. Unfortunately, some are in my own personal rearview mirror. While I—and others—have the best of intentions, I get sidetracked and become ineffective in progressing toward my destination.

Most often, some element of the details of ministry distracts me. Here are some examples of how excessive emphasis upon details have caused focus failure:

- The puppet ministry in our church put literally hundreds of hours into stage construction, décor, lighting and practice—but no one bothered to ask, "So what are we trying to accomplish spiritually here?" The script, written by the director, was lacking a spiritual message, and as a result, after the day of the show, the church leadership rightly questioned its purpose. *Focus failure!*

- If you are familiar with Awana, you know that we use game time in the elementary ages to attract kids. We have many training resources for all aspects of our ministry, and they are specific—

showing techniques that can make the game time highly efficient, exciting to kids and effective. But sometimes, our Awana people get too militant about the specifics. For example, our game time is usually divided into four teams designated by colors: red, blue, green, and yellow. I have observed our leaders getting upset if the colors aren't in the correct order: "Don't you know—the *proper* order is always by the length of the word (that only works in English)—and red is always on the north side of the game area." *Focus failure!*

- I visited a seminary classmate who had become a children's pastor. Diane and I spent the weekend with him, speaking to his children's workers and encouraging them. But during the weekend, I became deeply discouraged through my informal conversations with him. He was completely obsessed with a plan he had to redesign his children's ministry wing of the church. Several times during the weekend, I heard him say, "Everything our kids see in their world is of Disney quality—we need to be as entertaining and attractive as Disney in the church." That didn't concern me as much as his stumbling response when I asked him, "So what are you seeing happen in the lives of the kids in your ministry?" He couldn't tell me. It seemed his heart was all in the development of the building, but not at all connected with the spiritual development of the kids. *Focus failure!*

There was nothing wrong with his desire to have an attractive, first-rate environment, but it felt to me like it had distracted his focus away from the needs of the children. The problem was that he wasn't communicating the need for it with a ministry purpose.

Do you stay focused? Are you locked on to the needs of the children in your group? Are you constantly thinking—and praying—about how they will turn out as adults? Your ministry will be greatly enhanced if you do.

What Motivates You?

My friend Dr. Greg Carlson[2] says that some people are motivated by "what is," some by "what ought to be" and some by the process of how to get there. Some children's workers see the needs of the kids—"what is"—and are motivated by them. Others are visionary and see the distant vista of "what ought to be" in the children's future, and that motivates them. Some of us just want to get at it and do something.

Whichever way is your natural motivation, you will do well to keep focused on both "what is" and "what ought to be"—and you will have clearer direction for what you want to do.

What are the challenges?

- It is challenging to understand the needs of the children, especially when we see them for just a short time each week.

- It is easy to name the outcome we desire—that the children will be lifelong followers of Jesus Christ, but so difficult to know the path to get there and how we can help them along the way.

What to Do

Whatever our roles, we can implement the lessons from the story of the beggar at the gate, and from the life of Nehemiah. Here are some practical things you can do to get started.

- *Teachers and small-group leaders:* Determine that you will know the needs of the children you personally work with, as best you can. You may even want to use the chart on page 109 to organize your thoughts. Make every effort to build strong relationships with them and their parents so that you can better know where they are spiritually and in other areas of life.

- *Ministry leaders:* Keep your volunteers focused on that distant outcome. Talk about it, promote it and always encourage everyone to do his or her part.

- *Directors and pastors:* Talk to youth ministry. Start conversations about how you can align better for greater long-term effectiveness.

- *Curriculum selectors:* Think about the long term. Don't choose something just for a quarter or a year.

Earnestly pray for the future of your children. In addition to calling on the power of God in their lives, the activity of praying will help you stay focused on the current need.

Get your spiritual binoculars focused first on needs, then on the outcome, and then lock on to the target. You will accomplish so much more in children's ministry.

Notes

1. Larry Fowler, *Raising a Modern-Day Joseph* (Colorado Springs, CO: David C. Cook, 2009), pp. 53-54.
2. Dr. Greg Carlson is Chair of the Department of Christian Ministries at Trinity International University in Deerfield, Illinois.

IT'S NOT ENTIRELY
UP TO YOU

Aren't you glad that you have supernatural help in ministering to children? Rest in that truth for a few moments.

In both the story of the beggar by the gate and the building of the walls of Jerusalem, we see the power of God at work. While we can learn much from the perspectives and actions of Peter and John and Nehemiah, we are limiting our understanding of what drives ministry if we don't also recognize the supernatural intervention of God in the situation. In the story of Peter and John, God supernaturally intervened and healed the crippled beggar. Without that element, the story would be uninspiring at best. In the story of Nehemiah, we clearly see God-directed circumstances and events that allowed Nehemiah to achieve success in ministry.

God's help is clearly apparent in both biblical stories. I am certain it is also clear in your life. As a committed follower of Jesus Christ, you can look back and see God's work, can't you? He has used others to sense your need, minister to you and help you on your way to a life of devotion to Christ. Take a moment and thank the Lord for those who were perceptive enough to identify your need and point you to God's solution. Praise Him for those who saw a potential spiritual outcome in you and encouraged you toward it. And then direct your praise toward God, because it is ultimately His empowerment that made all of their efforts worthwhile.

So don't forget: It is not entirely up to us when we minister to others. God is with us. He will supply the power, and *that* is good reason for praise.

THE SIGNIFICANT "ONE"

The Right Organization of Children's Ministry

STANDARD 5:
We value every individual child and are concerned about not losing even one.

See that you do not look down on one of these little ones.
MATTHEW 18:10

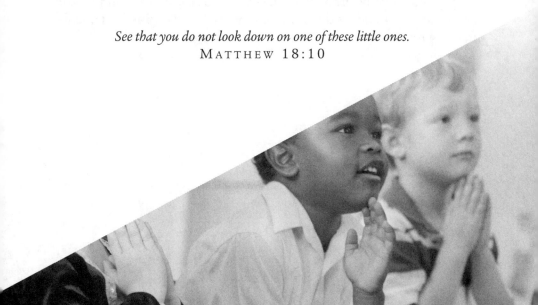

Hendrick Motorsports was our mystery destination. I was teaching during a training event for our key Awana leadership in Concord, North Carolina, and our training host was to plan a mystery trip for an outing. I have to confess, I knew very little about NASCAR racing engines before then (I still don't). But I learned a few things as a tour guide showed us around the plant:

- The engines are made completely of aluminum. They have to be really light for the cars they are put in to achieve maximum speed.

- They are made to last only six hours, then they are returned for either retooling or for melting down and starting over. In fact, our tour guide said, "If the engine lasts those six hours, we consider it a good engine." (I remember thinking, *I'm sure glad my Chevy Cavalier's engine lasts longer than that.*)

- Hendrick Motorsports only makes about 700 engines a year. The engines are not made for retail, but only to supply the race teams. Their goal is not to expand their business and make more. They care primarily about making those 700 engines last the six hours.

We also got to try changing the lug nuts like the professional racing teams do it. That was a lot of fun, but we were not nearly as fast as the pros.

During the tour, the guide said something that deeply impacted me—especially as I reflected on how it related to children's ministry: "We are not concerned about how many engines we *make*," he said, "we are only concerned about how many we *lose*. And last year was a good year—out of the 700 engines, we only lost 3." Then he showed us the décor around the factory—charts and slogans that affirmed they counted engines lost and were shooting for a perfect year. Their annual goal was to *not lose one.*

I wondered, *What if we thought like that in children's ministry?*

JESUS AND THE SIGNIFICANCE OF ONE

Jesus' Focus on One

I have been deeply impressed by Jesus' continued emphasis on the individual, and it comes through most clearly in the longest section in the Bible about children—in Matthew 18. The scene begins with Jesus calling a little child to Him (see v. 2) and using that child as a central focus for His teaching:

> At that time the disciples came to Jesus and asked, "Who is the greatest in the kingdom of heaven?" He called a little child and had him stand among them (Matt. 18:1-2).

Note that Jesus is using one child as an object lesson. Then, as His conversation with the disciples continues, there is repeated mention of the word or concept "one" in this passage.

Offending One

In Matthew 18:6, Jesus says, *"But if anyone causes **one** of these little ones who believe in me to sin, it would be better for him to have a large millstone hung around his neck and to be drowned in the depths of the sea"* (emphasis added).

Other translations render "to sin" as "to stumble." Both concepts are included in Jesus' meaning here. The warning is for anyone who causes a little child to stumble and fall in his or her spiritual journey.

I would feel much more comfortable if Jesus had said, "If anyone causes a *bunch* of these little ones to sin." Regrettably, I can think back over my ministry years and remember times when I was too harsh with a child or I didn't follow up with a child who quit coming. There have been times when my example wasn't the best. Am I guilty of causing a child to stumble? I don't think I've caused a bunch to stumble, but *one*—I want to say, "Jesus, that's a really high standard."

But Jesus is emphasizing His concern for people—and that includes even one little child.

Despising One

Jesus returns to the emphasis on "one" in verse 10, when He says, *"See that you do not look down on one of these little ones."*

Every children's ministry, even a small ministry, has at least one child that taxes one's sensitivities. We all have one child who stinks or won't obey or is loud or . . . (you fill in the description). I'm wondering if Jesus had that child in mind when He made the statement. The "one" in His statement is *so* significant. Think how it would read without it: "See that you do not look down on these little ones." In that case, it would be a warning against not liking children—and we could all say, "Not me! I passed on that issue!" But He didn't say it that way. He said, "Don't look down on *one*." Ouch. I confess. I've violated that admonition.

As I've matured, I've learned to see all children differently. One of my more recent "projects" was Damon.[1] When he first came, he was quick to get offended and would lash out—sometimes physically—at the other kids. When an adult corrected him, he would go sit up against a wall and sulk. It was a BIG temptation to look down on Damon—but Jesus said I was not to do that. So I gave myself the assignment of trying to value him and build him up. Other adults in our ministry did the same, and we began to see a change in Damon.

One day, he seemed especially cooperative and mature, and I determined to point it out. I said, "Damon, who picks you up?" Damon said "My dad." (It was actually his uncle who had rescued Damon from a drug-infested, abusive home and adopted him.) I said, "When he comes, please tell him I want to talk to him before you leave. I want to tell him how much you are maturing and how you have been a good example to the other kids." His face said he was pleased, and he promised to tell his dad.

Just a few minutes after we released the kids to go with their parents, Damon and his dad came up to me. "You wanted to talk to me about Damon?" I could hear the reluctance in the dad's voice.

"Yes, I want you to be aware of how we see Damon maturing. His behavior has been much improved and today he was a great example for the other kids. I wanted you to know it."

The dad's eyes glistened. "I've been talked to a lot about Damon's behavior," he said. "But this is the first time I've ever gotten a positive report like this." He gave Damon a big, BIG hug. Damon looked *so* pleased.

Ever since that time, Damon has been more mature, more responsive and well behaved. What if we adults had allowed ourselves to despise him? What would have happened?

My experience with Damon has reinforced the importance of what Jesus said: "Don't despise even one." Jesus said it. We need to obey.

Losing One

In Matthew 18:12-14, Jesus says, *"What do you think? If a man owns a hundred sheep, and **one** of them wanders away, will he not leave the ninety-nine on the hills and go to look for the **one** that wandered off? And if he finds it, I tell you the truth, he is happier about that **one** sheep than about the ninety-nine that did not wander off. In the same way your Father in heaven is not willing that **any** of these little ones should be lost"* (emphasis added).

I think it's fun sometimes to think of Scripture through the lens of "if Jesus were like us." If we do that in this case, here's how the parable might change:

> *If a man owns a hundred sheep, and one of them wanders away, will he not boast to the other shepherds about his excellent retention record? "I've got ninety-nine sheep," he says. "How many do you have?"*

Or maybe, if Jesus were like us, it might read like this:

> *If a man owns a hundred sheep, and one of them wanders away, will he not blame the one sheep for being so immature and uncommitted, and forget to go and look for the sheep?*

Here's another one:

> *If a man owns a hundred sheep, and one of them wanders away, will he not assume that another shepherd is caring for the one sheep that wandered off?*

Therefore, he will not venture into the mountains to find the one that was lost.

Aren't we glad that God is not like us? Yet, while the point of this parable is to reveal the heart of God for even one person (in this case a small child is in focus), we ought to be seeking to emulate Him in our role as shepherds of the flocks He has given us.

Look again at these three passages (vv. 6,10,12-14). Three cautions are made clear:

1. *CAUTION: Don't cause one little child to stumble spiritually* (v. 6). I unpacked this verse in chapter 5 of *Rock-Solid Kids*, which is titled "Avoiding the Millstone." Let me encourage you to read (or reread) that chapter; it is *vital* to follow this biblical mandate.

2. *CAUTION: Don't look down on one child.* Let me remind you, this was a dominant theme in Jesus' ministry. He was always willing to minister to the individual and was not deterred by the most repulsive of appearances and behavior. Think about this:

   • What could be more physically repulsive than a leper with all his deformities? Jesus *touched* him (see Mark 1:41).

   • What could be more disgusting than a naked, demon-possessed man? Jesus met him and ministered to him (see Mark 5).

   • Who could be more pitiful than a blind or crippled beggar? Jesus didn't avoid either one.

   • Who could more dangerous to the reputation of a spiritual leader than a suspected prostitute? Jesus didn't let that deter Him from ministering to the woman at the well (see John 4).

   The next time you are tempted to look down on a child, remember the despicable qualities of these biblical examples of real people that Jesus ministered to, and then respond the way He did.

3. *CAUTION: Don't lose even one* (see vv. 12-14). One more time, let me rewrite this parable—this time in kid-min terms:

What do you think? If a children's pastor has a hundred children in his ministry, and one of them wanders away, will he not leave the ninety-nine at the church and go to look for the one that wandered off? And if he finds him, I tell you the truth, he is happier about that one child than about the ninety-nine that did not wander off.

Do we do that? To answer, we probably need to first define what qualifies as "wandering away."

- A child whose family moves to another geographical location? Probably not, as that scenario is outside of your control and influence.

- A child who goes to another church? Probably not, as you will hope and pray the child will be shepherded there.

- A child who no longer goes to church? Probably yes, because unless his parents do it, there is no spiritual shepherd looking out for him. And it's most likely that parents who don't take their child to church will probably not do it at home.

"Wandering away" pictures a child no longer under the care of a spiritual shepherd. That's the definition I want you to consider.

The Potential of One

I have always loved the lyrics of the song "Shepherd Boy," in which the writer describes how Jesse called his sons to stand before the prophet Samuel so one of them would be chosen to be king of Israel. However, "No one thought to call [David]; surely he would never wear a crown."

The writer of these lyrics believed that Jesse may have felt that his youngest son, David, was not king potential and could be left out of the selection process. While Scripture doesn't tell us what Jesse was thinking (see 1 Sam. 16), it is pretty clear that he thought it was sufficient to bring the seven older sons and leave David at home. Maybe the youngest simply was not valued in that culture, or maybe it was something about David's personality that made his father think he didn't have king potential, or maybe David was just out in the fields when the invitation came and there wasn't time to go get him. Maybe Jesse thought, *Samuel said to bring my sons, and I've got all but one. And he is too young for this special invitation, so I'll just take the rest. It will be all right to leave just one at home.*

Whatever his thoughts, David was disregarded, and you know the rest of the story. The one who Jesse overlooked is the very one whom Samuel said God had selected to use. May I remind you that we never know which child that comes to our ministry might be one for whom God has great plans. May I also remind you that God has plans for *every* child who enters our doors.

I have loved reading *Finding Home,* the life story of Jim Daly, president of Focus on the Family. As an orphan who was bounced from foster home to foster home, he was certainly a candidate for being overlooked. I doubt that anyone would have dreamed that he would become such a fine leader of such a fine organization.

What is the possibility that there is a Jim Daly in your children's ministry program? Do you have a child with king potential, like David, who has not yet been invited? We dare not overlook even one, because we never know what God might do through him or her.

* * * * *

Do you have a shepherd's heart? I believe that the fact that you are reading this means that you do. I know that I do. However, this parable that Jesus shared of the shepherd and His sheep causes me to examine my own practice: Do I pursue a child who "wanders away" as diligently as the shepherd does in Jesus' parable?

I encourage you to reexamine your own pursuit of the individual child in your ministry. In the next chapter, we will discuss how to better avoid losing even one.

Note
1. Not his real name.

ORGANIZING FOR RETENTION

In your ministry, do like Hendrick Motorsports does in their business: Stop talking about how many you *have* and start focusing on how few you *lose*. Of course, we are talking about children, not race engines.

If you don't want your "sheep" to wander away, you have good cause to do three things: (1) be diligent in registration and recordkeeping, (2) structure for individual attention, and (3) envision for shepherding.

Diligent Registration and Recordkeeping

Henry was in my Awana club small group. Carlos brought him—Carlos attended our club regularly and invited Henry to come in order to complete his bring-a-friend requirement. Henry had just moved in down the street from Carlos. He was living with his grandmother because his mom "wasn't able to take care of him." Other than that, we didn't know anything about his home life. Henry *loved* coming to Awana. He was eager to learn and responsive. He didn't miss a session.

I remember the November 1 meeting that year. I remember it because it was the night after Halloween. On Halloween night a car hit the son of one of my co-workers while he was trick-or-treating. The car was speeding in a residential area, and it hit my friend's son hard enough to knock him about 30 feet. Incredibly—no, miraculously—he was not injured, just bruised. So I took the opportunity, since I was teaching the lesson that night, to tell the story and then ask, "What if it had been you? Are you ready to face eternity?"

I could see Henry's face during the lesson. He was listening intently and thinking about what I was saying. At the end, I asked, "If you are not sure about going to heaven, would you like me to pray for you?" I asked the kids to raise their hands if they wanted prayer. Henry raised his hand immediately, along with others.

I stayed afterward, because I had told the kids that if they wanted to talk more about salvation and eternity, I was available. Some approached me, and I hoped that Henry would too. But when I finished counseling the kids who did come, Henry was gone. *I'll talk with Henry next week*, I thought.

But Henry didn't come the next week. I didn't think much of it, but after he was absent the next week—and the next—I thought, *I'll see if I can call and find out what was the problem*. I asked for his registration card. To my dismay, there was no address on Henry's card. No phone number. No name of his grandma. No contact information at all. We had not been careful enough in registering Henry.

I knew that the only way to get in touch with Henry would be through Carlos and his parents. But that was a lot of extra work. And then I got busy . . . and I never asked them.

Henry wandered away and I didn't go look. I didn't know *where* to look, and I didn't try.

I deeply regret it to this day.

I intended to follow up, but the lack of adequate information was a barrier I didn't overcome.

Here's my point: If we want to keep our sheep from wandering away, we can start by making sure we have adequate information from their parents or guardians when they register. *The purpose for accurate registration procedures is not just to find out who comes and be prepared to minister to them, but also to minister to those who are absent by following up and loving them.*

Your Registration Process

There are many software packages available now and in use for the registration process, but Karl Bastian[1] suggests two low-tech solutions:

1. We print out the kids' names by grade and put the sheets out on a table. As they enter, they circle their name to show they are there. If their name isn't on the sheet, they fill out

a Guest Registration form. Later, the circled names and guest forms are entered into the church database for attendance.

2. Nametags of all regular kids are on a wall, by grade, in wall calendars with slots for each day (you can buy these at any teacher supply store) and each kid takes his or her nametag. Regular kids' nametags will be missing, and absent kids will remain. No nametag? Then fill out the guest form. As kids leave, they drop their nametags in a bucket—a different color for each grade. Later, a volunteer enters names from the nametags in the buckets and the guest forms into a database for attendance.

You will notice that in both of Karl's suggestions, there are two kinds of registration: regular weekly records of a child's presence, and an initial gathering of vital information (what he calls the Guest Registration form). Both are critical, but you also need to *do* something with each of them. We will look at that in a bit, but here is how Kris Smoll[2] does it:

Instead of reusable nametags, we use preprinted disposable nametags. (Tracking kids can all be done by names left on preprinted nametag sheets. Nametags that are left behind are absent children, names taken are present, and a class roster with highlighted/circled names are used only for tracking kids for the morning.) Class lists can be physically divided after class so that leaders can effectively pray for those who attended and for those who didn't attend. When leaders pray for kids, they become more focused on the kids' spiritual needs when present or not present.

The following questions will help you think through what you do once you gather the information. Questions concerning your registration process:

1. *Are you gathering adequate information?* In other words, are you thorough in gathering all the vitals on each child: full name and contact information of parent(s) or guardian? Proper permissions? Personal connections (who brought them or invited them)? In other words, do you have all the information you need to contact a parent or guardian if you need

to? Many children's ministries see this as the *end* of the need for registration—so they can contact the parents of a bawling baby or a kid that is puking. But there is so much more that you can do with registration information—and that you *need* to do with registration information.

2. *Do you track absenteeism?* Do you know what percentage of the children enrolled you would consider a "regular"? What is the percentage of regulars who are absent on any given Sunday? Do you know, or are you only tracking the positive bottom line of how many children are present? The better you watch the absenteeism, the better you will reflect God's attitude toward the one that wanders away.

3. *If a child is absent, do you have adequate procedures in place to encourage him or her to come back?* Are the children sent a reminder to return? In today's digital world, receiving a postcard or letter by snail mail becomes a unique event for most children and can be so effective in encouraging them to come back.

4. *Do you record why they were absent, if you find out?* Understanding why is extremely informative for the volunteer who works with the child, as well as for the director of the program, to analyze needs and effectiveness.

5. *If you have adequate information, and you have procedures in place to encourage absentees to come back, do you do it?* I have been guilty of establishing good procedures and then letting them lag. How about you? If we want to keep as many children as possible from wandering away, we will follow through to the end of the process with each one.

Ongoing Procedures and Recordkeeping

If we care about *each* individual child, we will also make sure that we are diligent in ongoing procedures. First of all, it is mandatory that we have *clear weekly check-in and checkout procedures* and then follow them. The danger of child predators and the potential for litigation, with the accompanying insurance requirements, are reasons enough.

Medium-sized churches and large ones do quite well at this. Let me especially caution those who are in small churches, because you know everyone personally, there is a temptation to allow your procedures to relax. That may be the thing that provides a sliver of opportunity for trouble to enter and injure your ministry. Make sure you *maintain* the standards and processes you set up.

Second, use your recordkeeping for ongoing measurements. Do you track regularity of attendance? Can you measure ministry effectiveness? Do you have a way to assess family impact? Each of those things can be enhanced through using the recordkeeping you do have.

There is a small detail that is often overlooked in the parable Jesus told: the shepherd *counted* the sheep. THAT is recordkeeping in the Bible. Let's do the same today and be diligent in the way we do it!

Structure for Individual Attention

If we are to share the heart of Jesus for the individual, it must be reflected in how we construct our ministries.

Here's the bottom line question: Are you able to minister to every child individually? Let me ask it another way: Are your volunteers able to build a close enough relationship with the children assigned to them that they can individually shepherd them?

In order to answer that well, you may need to consider your structure. I'm not going to discuss all structure possibilities in use today, but here are three examples that will demonstrate what I mean.

1. *The rotation method* (having children go from station to station) is effective in learning and minimizes the demands upon a volunteer, but it may not be the best way to build relationships. We want children to *learn*, but we also want them to be shepherded. Let's face it: if our volunteers only have a few minutes with children, they likely will not have many personal interactions with the individual kids. If you use the rotation method, adapt it or add to it so that your workers have an adequate opportunity to develop relationships with individual children.

2. *Large group ministry* is efficient and allows for good use of the giftedness of a few but may result in children being spectators rather than sheep. It is my observation that the larger the church, the more of a challenge this is and the

greater the temptation to just do large-group ministry. Even if you have a large-group approach, you must find a way to disciple children individually.

3. *Role/responsibility sharing* happens when, for example, volunteers serve one week a month. It is a structure that is abysmal at creating the environment necessary for shepherding. This approach results in the workers seeing their responsibility in terms of fulfilling the job description rather than relationship building and shepherding.

We've got to do better if we are going to "keep the sheep"! Here are some possible strategies for giving individual attention in the discipleship of children.

Strategy #1: Have the Parents Do It

This is best, of course, for a lot of reasons: (1) you maintain a great teacher-student ratio; (2) the teacher—in this case, the parent—has a pretty intimate knowledge of the child; (3) the teacher-parent already has a deep relationship with the student; (4) the teacher-parent can also see if the spiritual truths taught are being lived out, and he or she can reinforce and re-teach as necessary.

My friend Kris Smoll has been intentional about engaging parents. Here are some things she said they do in her church:

- We invite a parent into the classroom as a special guest, as a helper who brings in a snack or unique prop that matches the lesson or to be a substitute helper for one week. This will introduce them to what is done in a classroom and hopefully ignite a passion for teaching and leading their kids spiritually in the class and at home.

- We also gather emails or create a closed Facebook group where only parents of those in the classroom can have access. This accomplishes several things: (1) Parents can connect with what was taught in class to create interest and connection in the class; (2) when the child's teacher builds a relationship with the parents (or guardians), it leads toward dramatically improving the attendance; and (3) it also builds excitement/anticipation and paints a vision of what is coming, which helps keep the excitement of attending class alive.

- We love taking weekly photos (photo release needed) of what happens in the class and send it out to the involved families to view.

- We also take time to build up the volunteers in the communications so that when needs arise folks are quick to get involved because they know it will be fun, encouraging and they will serve with other people they know.

All of us in children's ministry aspire to have the parents do it as much as possible. After all, it is *biblical*. It is also *best*. But we also know reality: Many parents either don't know how or aren't motivated enough to do it. That means we need a second strategy to supplement what the parents do.

Strategy #2: Shepherd the Children in Small Groups

This provides something every Christian parent should welcome—the influence of another godly adult in his or her children's lives. The shepherding that goes on in children's ministry is supplemental rather than primary for kids from Christian homes, but it is primary for those from non-Christian homes. Without an opportunity for strong personal relationships, which comes through groups that are small in number, true shepherding becomes difficult.

Why small groups? We often promote small groups in ministry (even in children's ministry) for the purpose of community. But I suggest there is a strong reason to have small groups (groups that are small in number) so that the group leader can minister to (shepherd) the individual child.

It isn't practical to expect a one-to-one ratio between the volunteer "shepherd" and the children, is it? But small groups—groups of five or fewer children—provide a great opportunity to influence the children through community and also through shepherding. Small groups create the environment where the group leader will begin to feel ownership of the relationships with the children, which then leads to a more shepherding attitude.

Try a test: Print out a list of the children (you SHOULD have one) that attend your ministry. Shut your eyes. Put your finger on the paper, then open your eyes. Ask yourself, *Is this child that my finger is pointing to being shepherded in a godly, personal relationship with an adult?*

Or is that child just "part of the herd"?

During my years of working with churches in the Los Angeles area, I regularly (just about every week) observed children's ministries—most of them Awana clubs. I confess that the impressions run together and I can't remember too many specific situations except the really bad ones.

One really bad one had to do with this issue of structure. It was my practice to observe while walking around with a director or church leader and then give suggestions afterward. I recall this one instance, though, as we were going into the preschool area to observe the Cubbies (the Awana ministry for the four- and five-year-olds) group. "This isn't going to look very good," the director apologized ahead of time. "Really? Why?" I wanted to know. "We're really short of leadership. We've got 42 cubbies and only 3 leaders. Don't expect much." I knew it wouldn't look pretty, and it didn't. The three frazzled volunteers were not able to do much more than baby-sit and do crowd control. Needless to say, the purpose of the ministry was not being carried out.

It wasn't that the leadership wanted it that way. They said, "We just can't get anyone to help." Wow! Have I heard that line repeated over and over again! Maybe you are thinking, *That is our situation too.*

So what is the answer? Make sure that you are recruiting to a vision, not an empty position. In fact, it would be good to review the "recruiting pitch" to Jason on page 90. It works pretty well with both men and women. Determine that in recruiting, you will set an expectation that "we will set-tle for nothing but the best in shepherding, and that means quality small groups with manageable ratios."

Envision for Shepherding

Volunteers are generally reluctant to see themselves as a "shepherd." Either they aren't sure what it means or they are aware of their own inadequacies and are not sure they qualify to "lead" the sheep. As a result, it is important to reset their viewpoint and then equip them for shepherding. Here are two basic shepherding principles.

A Shepherd Is Responsible for His Sheep

When nineteenth-century evangelist Dwight L. Moody was starting out in ministry, he had an irrepressible heart for children. I've always been impressed with the following story:

It was not long after he came to Chicago that he began to work among the children. His success in recruiting for the Sunday schools was wonderful. On one occasion he found a little mission Sunday school on the North side, and offered to take a class. The superintendent pointed out that they already had almost as many teachers as pupils, but added that, if Mr. Moody would get his own pupils, he would be at liberty to conduct a class. The next Sunday Mr. Moody appeared with eighteen ragamuffins. They were dirty, unkempt, many of them barefoot, but as the young teacher said, "each had a soul to save."[3]

A Sunday School teacher going out and *finding* his own class? It is unheard of today, but the story remains a vivid example of a shepherd's heart. It is vital that a teacher feels ownership for his or her sheep.

"My kids." Do you hear your volunteers use that phrase to refer to their small group? Do you hear conversations that tell you they feel responsible for the spiritual growth of specific children? If you do, it is evidence that they have the vision to be a shepherd.

A Shepherd Must Know His Sheep by Name

This is how Jesus describes a shepherd: *"He calls his own sheep by name"* (John 10:3). You've seen pictures of flocks of sheep—to someone unfamiliar with the flock, they look exactly the same, without distinction. To differentiate one sheep from another is impossible to all but the shepherd, but it is the *job* of a shepherd. How does a shepherd identify sheep that look identical to one another? You know the answer: by spending so much time with them that even the slightest differences in looks, mannerisms or behavior becomes apparent.

Volunteers must be encouraged—and equipped—to get to know the children. You can equip them by how you structure your ministry: You create time for them to get to know those assigned to them, equip them by providing the information you acquire through registration, and create simple getting-to-know you questionnaires they can use with the children.

They also will get to know their sheep as they follow the practical advice I gave in the "Seven Ways to Impact Thinking" chapter: encourage them to become question-askers rather than advice-givers. Often we think that leading children means that we must have great answers for them, whether they ask a question or not. Instead, asking "why," "how," or "what do you think" questions gives us an opportunity to know not only what the children are thinking but how to respond to them and lead them more effectively.

A Challenge

You are probably familiar with statistics that tell us we are losing young people once they become young adults. That is a great concern to me, and I am sure it is to you as well. But let's not lose them when they are still in our "flock." Even if we keep 99, let's be concerned that we not lose even one.

Will you take it as a challenge? Stop focusing on how many you have and start being concerned about not losing even one. Practice these steps:

- Keep records.
- Analyze what happens with the children under your care.
- Know why they don't come back.
- Do something about it when you can.

If you do these things, you will better reflect the heart of God.

Notes

1. Karl Bastian is founder and president of Kidology, and a walking children's ministry encyclopedia.
2. Kris Smoll is director of Children's Ministry at Appleton Alliance Church in Appleton, Wisconsin.
3. Rev. J. Wilbur Chapman, *The Life and Work of Dwight Lyman Moody*, 1900. Available online at http://www.biblebelievers.com/moody/06.html.

FEEL RIGHT

JESUS CARES FOR *YOU*

Jesus cares for you, doesn't He? Aren't you glad for the way God values you as an *individual*? Let me remind you of two more passages that speak of the importance of one:

> *Are not two sparrows sold for a penny? Yet not **one** of them will fall to the ground apart from the will of your Father. . . . You are worth more than many sparrows* (Matt. 10:29,31, emphasis added).

Jesus' point is that even a sparrow is significant to God, but each of us as individuals are even more important to Him. Take a minute to bask in the personal attention and care that God gives you and be reminded that He also feels the same about every single child in your ministry.

> *And if anyone gives even a cup of cold water to **one** of these little ones because he is my disciple, I tell you the truth, he will certainly not lose his reward* (Matt. 10:42, emphasis added).

Jesus spoke about just *one* cup of water to *one* little child. What is Jesus' point? That even the smallest gesture of love to a child is significant in ministry.

Just one. In God's sight, *one* is a very significant number.

POWER TRIANGLE

The Right Power in Children's Ministry

STANDARD 6:
We know where spiritual power comes from and rely upon it to fuel our ministry.

I am not ashamed of the gospel, because it is the power of God.
ROMANS 1:16

It was 1992. I was in Almaty, the capital of Kazakhstan (at the time), on the other side of the world. A team that I led had planted the Awana ministry there earlier, and three of us, along with a translator, had returned to assess progress and see if we could provide further direction.

Because there were few hotels, we stayed in a mission house belonging to a church. It was like a bed-and-breakfast. Our two cooks were young ladies, Anya and Zarema. Both were about 20. Anya was of Russian descent, and Zarema was Kazakh. Zarema was from a Muslim family, but had become a Christian. About the second day of our visit, she told us that her parents wanted to invite us to their home for a meal. We accepted, and though I was nervous about being in a Muslim home for the first time, it was a wonderful experience.

Later in the evening, we were to be driven back to the mission house. There were too many in our party to fit in one car, so the Muslim dad offered to help transport us. I got in his car, along with the translator, David (pronounced Da-VEED), and Anya and Zarema. As we were traveling back, the translator said to me, "They are talking about stopping at a hospital. Anya's younger sister is a patient there."

We went into a dark stairwell in the hospital and walked up one flight to a second floor, then down a hallway to a plain lobby area. Within a minute or so, a middle-aged lady came and sat with us, along with a young girl who appeared to be about 12. The girl was very weak and had to be supported while they walked. I understood that this was Anya's mother and young sister—who was the one that was sick.

They all started talking together in hushed tones, in Russian. The ladies were all teary-eyed, and the Muslim dad was trying to console them. I felt out of place. But being a people person, I didn't want to just sit there. So I asked David, the translator, "What's wrong with the little girl?" and he relayed my question to the mother. He translated her answer: "She says that Natalia has a cancer in her chest. She has heard they can cure this cancer in the United States, but they can't do it here."

I didn't know how to respond to the last part. I was the only American. Do I say, "That's too bad," or "I'm sorry," and leave it at that? I didn't know how I could help either. I had never thought about bringing someone to the United States. I felt so uncomfortable—and so inadequate. So without having a clue about how I might do it, I just said, "Well, I'll try to help if I can."

The mom and Anya, when they heard what I said, broke into sobs. "*Spasibo, spasibo*," ("thank you" in Russian) they said over and over. I tried to back their hopes down a notch: "I just said I would try. I don't know if

I can do anything or not." I left the hospital that night thinking, *What have I gotten myself into?*

I did have enough sense to ask the mom to ask the doctor for a letter that would explain his diagnosis and what they had been doing to treat the girl. About two days later, while we were still staying at the mission house, Anya brought the letter to me, and I had David translate it into English. He didn't know medical terms in English, so it was really rough. (I remember that the kind of cancer wasn't even translated, but there was something about a "shining in the chest") Every time Anya would see me the tears would come again. "*Spasibo,*" she would say through her tears. So I had the letter but not a clue what I was going to do.

I arrived back home in late afternoon, and the first thing I did was to call our family doctor, who was a believer, and I read the letter to him. Then I asked, "Do you know what kind of cancer this is?" He said he did. "Is it curable in the U.S.?" He said, "Yes, with treatment it is." That answer made me feel really bad. Suddenly, I felt the weight of this little girl's life on my shoulders. *I had never felt that before.* I almost wished he had said, "No, it's not curable here"—because then I would have been off the hook.

"So what do I do?" I asked him. He didn't know—he was as clueless as I was. He had never helped someone come here from another country. "Who might know?" I asked. He told me that he thought either Children's Hospital or City of Hope (both in Los Angeles) might be able to help.

The next morning, I called City of Hope. I thought, *With that name, they ought to help.* I got transferred from person to person, and each time I explained the situation and read the letter. Finally, the person on the other end of the phone line was the right one and told me, "If you can raise the money to get her here, and for her treatment, then we will give you an application and consider her." I asked how much money that would be. Her answer was, "At least six figures." *One hundred thousand dollars?* My heart sank. I didn't think it was possible for me to raise that kind of money—especially in time to save the little girl. It sounded hopeless.

My doctor had also said to check with Children's Hospital, so I decided to call them too. I got transferred around the same way, read the letter a few more times and again finally found the person who could give me answers. The response was the same: "You raise the money, then we will consider an application." I thought I was at a dead end. Then, almost as an afterthought, the lady on the other end said, "Let me transfer you to the oncology department. Let's see if they have any ideas." So once more I was put on hold, once more I heard a new voice, and I told my story and read the letter.

When I finished, the lady on the other end said, "Well, you may not know it, but the director of our department is Dr. Stuart Siegel, and he is considered one of the world's leading experts in treating that kind of cancer. *He is traveling to the Soviet Union in two weeks, and he will be looking for patients to treat free of charge. Can she be there?"*

She gave me the address where he would be. I got off the phone and began calling Kazakhstan. It took more than 100 tries before I got through to an English speaker, but I finally did. *And just three weeks after first seeing her, Natalia was being treated by one of the best doctors in the world—completely free of charge.*

That was GOD! I can't explain it any other way but that God chose to move circumstances to preserve that little girl's life. I was clueless, powerless, without experience or understanding how to proceed. There was nothing I could depend upon but God doing something miraculous. And He did!

It wasn't quite the end of the story. I didn't hear, for a long time, what happened—until about 10 years later, when I saw Zarema again. She had married a pastor and was living in New Delhi, India. I met them for lunch, and I was so anxious to hear the rest of the story. She told me that Natalia was completely restored to health and was engaged to be married. But she also told me that her father was impressed enough that we tried to help that he wanted to help too—and he paid for the little girl's transportation to the clinic (it included a plane flight). Through it all, several members of Zarema's family have become believers in Jesus.

If someone were to ask me, "When have you really seen God's power at work through you?" I would tell that story. There are others—many others—but that one was a milestone in my life. I learned how incredibly, astonishingly awesome it is to be in a position where you get to see God's power displayed in or through you.

Have you ever seen it? Do you regularly see God at work? Do you sense His power?

Children's ministry workers need a reminder about its importance, don't we? That is the intent of this section: to *remind*. Are you ready?

SPIRITUALLY POWERED MINISTRY

I Missed It

I still have to be constantly reminded about the need to seek spiritual power in my ministry with kids, even though I have personally experienced God doing some amazing things. I had two recent experiences that demonstrated to me that I still forget what is important.

Last year in the Awana Club in my church, I was responsible for what we called a "Reward Room." When the kids completed their work in their small groups, they could choose to come into my room. There I was to lead them in activities that were both fun and productive, and we did a mixture of review and recall of what they had learned with simple games and challenges. It was to be low-key and fairly unstructured, but I wanted to do my best.

One week, I got really pumped up about a new game I had learned from the *Minute to Win It* TV show. I thought it would work well with a review of the books of the Bible. I put time and preparation into getting props, designing visuals and organizing how it was to be done—in fact, I put *all* my preparation time into those things. Then the club meeting came, and things just didn't go well at all. The kids weren't that engaged. They got more into the game than the review—in fact, they got *too* much into the game and started arguing over who should be doing what. It was pretty much a disaster as far as reviewing what they had learned. I beat myself up afterward:

Larry, you're supposed to be a children's ministry veteran, I told myself. *You can do better than this.* But I didn't put my finger on what went wrong until the next week.

That next week, everything went wrong with my prep time—meaning it pretty much disappeared. I had emergencies come up that took my time, I had a couple of days I felt sick, and I ended up with no time to prepare any new activities or develop any props. I thought, *I'll just have to repeat what we did last week,* and I felt guilty for not preparing well. On the way to Club, I prayed, "Lord, You know what my week has been like. You're going to have to help me tonight if anything positive gets accomplished." You guessed it—it was an amazing night. The game started off better than the previous week, and then as the kids were in the middle of playing—totally unexpectedly—one of them asked, "Mr. Larry, what is Job about?"

"As soon as we complete this set I'll tell you," I responded. And when we got to a stopping point, I told him briefly the story of Job. As soon as I was done, another one asked, "What is Nehemiah about?"

"Does anyone know?" I responded. I wanted to draw all of them into the discussion. Suddenly, this impromptu session caught the attention of all the kids. They were all listening and began to contribute with enthusiasm, and it ended up to be a simply amazing time of interacting and learning. I even felt the chills, thinking, *This is "God time!"* I went home afterward so pleased that God had worked in the kids' lives that night.

Can you identify? Have you ever put your heart and soul (and sweat) into preparation, only to have a disaster of a lesson? Then—at another time, with inadequate time for preparation, you have an experience that can only be explained as "Wow—that was God at work"?

What makes the difference? Is lack of preparation better? Of course not! What made the difference, I believe, was on Whom I was depending for power.

While depending upon God for power is essential in every ministry, the temptation to forget it is huge in children's work. Why? Because of all the "things" that are a part of what we do: media, visuals, object lessons, structure, stories, fun—all of those things can pull us away from relying on God's power to do our ministry.

Spiritually Powered Ministry

So, do you want a first-rate children's ministry (from all human perspectives) that is devoid of God's power? Or do you want a first-rate one that is *filled* with God's power? Not a hard choice, right? In fact, it is an easy choice, but knowing how to make it happen is a lot harder. To start, let's clearly *identify from Scripture* how His power fuels our ministry.

When I looked for the verses that specifically mentioned God's power at work through what we either said, thought or did, I found four clear principles that can lead to extraordinary power that in particular, are important for us who work with kids.

To help you remember them, I am visualizing them in a "Spiritual Power Triangle." What? Four parts in a triangle? Yes—the three sides and the interior. The three sides of the triangle answer three critical questions regarding opening the way for spiritual power to be applied in ministry:

- What can I do?
- What can I think?
- What can I say?

The Method of Spiritual Power: Earnest Prayer

If you are oriented to practicality, and you want to know right up front, "What can I do to fill my ministry with God's power?" here is your answer: PRAY. Yes, you know this to be a biblical truth. But, if you mirror what I have observed in children's workers I know, you don't live it very well in your ministry—and neither do those who work with you.

I've heard it said that if you want to kill a regular meeting of your ministry staff, just announce, "We are going to meet weekly for prayer." It's just about guaranteed that attendance will dwindle to a few in a very short period of time. Why is that? The very thing that will empower our ministries to be used mightily of God is the thing we push down the priority list.

Do you feel like I'm being too harsh? Then let me ask some questions:

- *Do* you pray for your children's ministry role each week?
- *Is* prayer an intentional part of your preparation?
- *Do* the volunteers who serve with you have a pattern of praying for the children individually?
- *Do* you have a ministry team prayer time, and if so, how good is the attendance?
- What is the prayer time like? *Does* it mirror what Scripture says prayer should be like?

Let's establish the truth God tells us in His Word: There is *power* in prayer. I love the way James 5:16 is translated in the *New Living Translation:*

The earnest prayer of a righteous person has great power and wonderful results.

"Great power and wonderful results." That's what I want in my ministry, don't you? If those two things come through earnest prayer, why don't we do it all the time?

Wait—sometimes we do. Sometimes when I am in a position of dependence I will get earnest in prayer. But when I am not in that position, I fail to be so earnest in prayer. Remember my story earlier in the chapter about my Reward Room? The difference between the two nights was that the second night I was dependent upon *God,* while on the first night I was dependent upon my *preparation.* When I was more dependent upon my preparation, my prayer, I must confess, was not so earnest. That is the first qualifier in James 5:16.

The second qualifier is *"the earnest prayer of a righteous person."* In John 9:31, Jesus said, *"We know that God does not listen to sinners. He listens to the godly man who does his will."* Earnest prayer by godly people—that is the activity that brings spiritual power. It is so simple but so easily forgotten or pushed aside. Is earnest prayer by godly people part of your children's ministry?

**Prayer must be earnest
in order to bring great power.**

I posted the following question on CMConnect: "Is anyone out there having success in getting their volunteers to participate in a prayer time for their ministry (even if it is a short one)?" I was searching for those who were finding consistency in earnest prayer by godly people. I especially appreciated these responses:

> Every week we have a prayer team that travels around to each of our departments and prays with each of our volunteers for that service. It goes over great for us and is a time the volunteers look forward to. —Todd McKeever

> Prayer is important, and it's our first step we take in the mornings. I know our church intercessors also make rounds and pray over every room, area and leader, no matter what. I tend to find that during kids' church I look up and one of them is standing in the back praying while I preach. I'm telling you, I love that. —Jenn Vintigni

Don't both scenarios sound like earnest prayer by godly people? In the next chapter, you will learn how you can make it a reality in your children's ministry as well.

Why don't we pray more? I believe it's because we are not practicing the second biblical power principle: *God's power shows more clearly through our weakness.*

The Mindset of Spiritual Power: Weakness

The apostle Paul was recounting his own experiences when he wrote:

> *But he said to me, "My grace is sufficient for you, for my power is made perfect in weakness." Therefore I will boast all the more gladly about my weaknesses, so that Christ's power may rest on me. That is why, for Christ's sake, I delight in weaknesses, in insults, in hardships, in persecutions, in difficulties. For when I am weak, then I am strong (2 Cor. 12:9-10).*

Notice two things: First, *a position of weakness is a cherished position.* It is impossible to read Paul's statement and come to a different conclusion: "boast gladly about" and "delight in" weaknesses? Wow! That is so different from how we normally react to a situation in which we are weak.

Second, *there is power in weakness.* Possibly the most difficult lesson I have learned in ministry was Paul's last statement: *"When I am weak, then I am strong."* Why is there power in weakness? Because when we are weak, we are more dependent upon God. When we are dependent upon God, then He releases His power through us.

These first two principles are interlocking: *Staying in a dependent position is key to practicing earnest prayer.* When I am not feeling so dependent, I am less likely to discuss my ministry endeavors with God.

Staying in a position of weakness, however, is not so easy. Here are some observations I have about this principle:

- People hate to be weak—especially men. We pray for strength, for health, for smooth sailing—but the truth is, God chooses to work most powerfully through those times when life is tough. Just answer this question: "When have you grown the most in your Christian life?" As I have asked that of others, the answer I almost always get back is a story about a most difficult time. So why do we pray the way we do?

- The longer you are in ministry and the more experienced you get, the greater the enticement to trust in your own abilities or expertise rather than stay dependent on God. The more we know what to do, the bigger the temptation to just do it and forget to ask God for His blessing and power. A caveat here: Let's not forget that experience is a gift from God, and He is the source of that as well.

Don't forget to stay *dependent.* It is a secret to seeing God's power displayed in your ministry!

A Personal Illustration

It was time for something different. We had been conducting our Awana Olympics (we have since changed the name to Awana Games) in smaller venues throughout the Los Angeles area. But I felt that our ministry in the L.A. area needed freshening, and a larger event, with all areas working together, would provide the means to refocus.

We rented Pauley Pavilion, the UCLA basketball arena, and began making plans to have a special day of competition and ministry to parents. Our plan was for 4,000 children to participate, and we hoped for an audience of 6,000 parents.

I wanted to get the best speaker I could find for the event, and I had someone in mind: A. C. Green. A. C. was a forward for the Los Angeles Lakers, and a committed Christian. He was deeply respected by the whole Los Angeles community for his play, but even more for his stand on sexual abstinence. A. C. was not afraid to proclaim that he was a virgin (quite rare for a pro basketball player), and he intended to stay that way until he married—all because of his faith in Christ.

I didn't know how to contact him. I knew no one in the Laker organization, and I had no connections, so I decided to just take a letter to the receptionist in the Laker's front office. The lady promised to pass it on to A. C.'s secretary, and I prayed it would happen. That was October.

By early December, I had heard nothing, so I tried to follow up. After leaving messages several times, I finally talked to the receptionist, who said, "A. C.'s secretary just picked up the mail." Our event was in March, and I was starting to get nervous. By mid-December, still no word, and the Lakers team went on a road trip through the holidays. On the Thursday after New Year's Day, I called the secretary and asked if A. C. had an answer yet. "No," she said. "He hasn't seen the mail yet. But he's coming in the office tomorrow, so I will make sure he sees your request. But don't get your hopes up—he has a game the night before and the day after. I'm almost positive he won't do it."

My heart sank. I had a staff training day scheduled for that Saturday, and I was so hoping to be able to announce that A. C. would be the speaker. Instead, I would have to ask people to pray—because if A. C. was to come, God was going to have to intervene. That Saturday, we had 975 people come for the staff training. It was going to be a huge event! We started the training by dividing everyone into prayer groups, and I gave them a list of things to pray for. One of them was that A. C. would accept our request to be the special guest speaker.

I felt in a position of weakness—of dependence. If A. C. was going to say yes, then God would need to display His power to make it happen. There was nothing else we could do except earnestly pray.

That night, about midnight, I got a call from Rick, one of my ministry team members. He said, "Larry, I'm so sorry for calling this late, but I wanted to let you know what happened tonight. Wadell (one of his volunteers—a high school senior, and a godly young man—perhaps, the best ambassador we could have selected from all 975 staff members) was on a date tonight and was sitting in a restaurant with his girlfriend when A. C. Green walked in and sat in the booth right next to him! Wadell went over to him and said, 'Hey, A. C.! I hear you're thinking about speaking at our Awana Olympics.'

A. C. responded, 'Yeah, I saw a letter about that last night. What is that?' Wadell told him all about it. They talked for about 20 minutes, and at the end of the time, A. C. said he'd do it." Rick added, "I thought you wouldn't mind my waking you up for that news." Believe me, I didn't mind at all!

When I was in a position of weakness—total dependence upon God to work—and when we had committed the issue to earnest prayer, He chose to display His power and cause the right connection at the right time with the right person. In my view, that was nothing but God at work!

On Monday morning, the secretary called. "A. C. came in this morning and told me to tell you he'd be happy to speak at your event. I'm surprised, but anyway, he is coming." She didn't know what I knew.

The day of the event came, and God greatly used it. A. C. gave his testimony so clearly and powerfully. He got a standing ovation that I thought was never going to end. At the end of the day, we read all the response cards—and on them, more than 60 parents indicated that they had put their faith in Jesus Christ that day.

Our Los Angeles area ministry needed a return to a position of dependence upon God, and the changes we made caused us to do that very thing. Let me ask you: Does your ministry need to return to a position of dependence? Then what might you do to cause that to happen?

A position of weakness is a great place to be. Add to that position the activity of earnest prayer and you've got two parts of the secret to spiritual power in your ministry. Let's look at the third part.

The Message with Spiritual Power: The Gospel

Look at these "power verses" in Scripture:

> I am not ashamed of the gospel, **because it is the power of God** for the salvation of everyone who believes: first for the Jew, then for the Gentile (Rom. 1:16, emphasis added).

> For Christ did not send me to baptize, but to preach the gospel—not with words of human wisdom, lest the cross of Christ be emptied of its power. For the message of the cross is foolishness to those who are perishing, but to us who are being saved **it is the power of God** (1 Cor. 1:17-18, emphasis added).

These verses connect the power of God with a *message*. We have seen that spiritual power is connected with a mindset (weakness or dependence) and with a method (the earnest prayer of godly people). Now we find the third part of the power triangle: the *gospel*. This is the part that has to do with what we *say*.

Again—this applies to all ministries, but we can't forget that in children's ministry it is critical that we rely on the right *message* for power.

What Message Has Spiritual Power?

What is the message that, when you communicate it, you can have confidence it is filled with spiritual power? At times, I have wished that Romans 1:16 would have said, "Larry's words are the power of God." But it doesn't say that; it says *the gospel* is the power of God. But *what is* the gospel?

Paul makes it clear in 1 Corinthians 15: It is the message of the death, burial and resurrection of Jesus.

> *Now, brothers, I want to remind you of the gospel I preached to you, which you received and on which you have taken your stand. . . . For what I received I passed on to you as of first importance: that Christ died for our sins according to the Scriptures, that he was buried, that he was raised on the third day according to the Scriptures* (vv. 1,3-4).

In verse 1, Paul tells the Corinthians he is going to remind them what the gospel is, and then he does it in verses 3 and 4. Look at what is packed into these simple phrases:

- *"Of first importance"*: The priority of this message. "First importance" here can mean "of highest priority." There are major implications for children's ministry in just this one thought.

- *"Christ died for our sins"*: The deity and messiahship of Jesus Christ, His atonement on our behalf, and man's sinful nature.

- *"According to the Scriptures"*: The reliability of the message and the fulfillment of Old Testament prophecy.

- *"That he was buried"*: The humanity of Jesus and the reality of His death.

- *"That he was raised on the third day"*: The deity of Jesus, the spiritual victory and the hope of resurrection

There is so much contained in this simple statement, but it is the *message* of power. It is also the core message of Christianity—the foundational truth for everything else we believe and teach. Do you agree? Is it core? Is it foundational? Then it ought to enjoy a prime place in our children's ministry curriculum, shouldn't it?

We Blow It

Yes, there is incredible spiritual dynamite in those simple truths. Yet, as children's ministry workers (me included), we are at times guilty of the following missteps.

We overshadow it with all the other things we teach. We teach Bible stories but fail to connect them with the Core Story. We teach virtues but fail to emphasize the victory over sin. We teach for spiritual growth but overlook spiritual birth. If there is anything our children must learn—and learn well—it is the simple gospel message of 1 Corinthians 15:3-4. If there is any Scripture passage that children ought to memorize, it is this one (okay—along with John 3:16). If there is any truth that needs to be deeply embedded into their thinking, it is the truth of the gospel.

We also fail to rely upon the spiritual power that is contained in the message of the gospel. We think our words are better. We think we may need to "help out" the message, so we rush through Bible passages or don't even use them at all—but we put lots of emphasis upon what we think or say.

We are so familiar with the gospel message that we have lost our awe of it. Let's not forget—the gospel is the Most Important Message in the world! It is also the Most Powerful Message in the world. We cannot allow our wonder to wane just because we have heard it so many times—and neither can we allow that to happen with the children we lead. Do you speak to the children you shepherd with wonder in your voice and face about the gospel? Do you speak *repeatedly* with wonder?

We can fail to remember that the gospel is transformational. That is much easier to see when a 36-year-old, who has lived a life of sin up to this point, finds Christ. It is more difficult to remember when a well-behaved six-year-old trusts Christ. But the transformation is not first behavioral, it is spiritual, and it is just as real in the child as it is in the adult.

My father-in-law, Ed Lindsay, is a living testimony to the transformational power of the gospel in the life of a young child. When he was small, a neighborhood family began taking him with them to church where he heard the gospel and was saved. The resulting transformation was genuine. I don't know if others in his family could see the difference when he was young, but God changed his heart. For many years, he was the only believer in his family, but he was unmoved by his difficult environment. He went through his teenage years desiring to live for God, and he married a believer (my mother-in-law, Leah). Together, they have established a legacy that is different from his past: Their children and grandchildren are all following God because of Ed and Leah's influence.

When did the transformation take place? When Dad was a little boy. Maybe it wasn't as dramatic as an adult's life-change upon receiving Christ, but it was no less real. Let's not forget that the truth of the gospel *transforms* lives.

The Bible gives us one more key to spiritual power: the Holy Spirit.

Power Comes Through the Holy Spirit

In 1 Thessalonians 1:5, Paul writes, *"Our gospel came to you not simply with words, but also with power, with the Holy Spirit and with deep conviction."*

This verse is a reminder that a display of spiritual power in my ministry is God's prerogative, not mine. There are no simple formulas. If you pray fervently and put yourself in position where you are dependent upon God, and you strongly proclaim the message of the gospel, it is still the Holy Spirit's decision to display awesome spiritual power or not.

We can't try to manipulate God and say, "God, I've prayed, I'm dependent upon You, and I'm proclaiming Your Word. So I expect a miracle here."

But the Holy Spirit—God in us—is the key. We pray for the Holy Spirit to empower us, we depend upon the Holy Spirit to strengthen us, and we trust in the Holy Spirit to use the message of the gospel to transform lives. But how does the Holy Spirit empower our ministry? There is an answer in the progression of thought in Ephesians 3.

First, the apostle Paul prays for the power of the Holy Spirit to be at work in the inner being of the believers in the Ephesian church:

> *I pray that out of his glorious riches he may strengthen you with power through his Spirit in your inner being* (Eph. 3:16).

Then, four verses later, Paul draws attention to the power of the Holy Spirit in His work through us:

> *Now to him who is able to do immeasurably more than all we ask or imagine, according to his power that is at work within us* (v. 20).

Do you see it? We want the first part of the verse to be true—we want God to *"do immeasurably more than all we ask or imagine."* But we forget that such a display of power is linked with—*"according to"*—the last part of the verse: *"his power that is at work within us."* How much the Holy Spirit will display His power *through* us is according to how His power is at work *in* us. Often, we want the first without yielding to the second.

Do you see evidence of spiritual power in your children's ministry? Do you want to? It begins inside you—it begins where you *think*. It begins with your mind being renewed, as Romans 12:1-2 tells us. When you begin to think scripturally about spiritual power, you will begin to act accordingly. Then spiritual power will be unleashed through you—at the Holy Spirit's prerogative—in ministry.

THE PATH TO POWER

How We Miss It

As a children's worker, there have been times when I have put my reliance on the wrong things. Here are the errors I have made. Maybe you can identify.

- *Relying on my own words.* Have you ever heard a preacher rush through reading a Scripture passage, then say something like this? "Now . . . (big pause) listen carefully . . ." When I hear that, I think, *Didn't you want everyone to listen carefully when you read the Scripture?* But I'm ashamed to admit I have done the same thing. I, too, often view *my* words as more noteworthy than God's Word. *Shame on me.*

- *Relying on massive preparation.* When I am a speaker, often someone will ask me before I begin, "Well, are you ready?" I understand their question to mean, "Is the media piece you are going to use tested and ready to go? Are your thoughts clear? Do you have your notes?" But I don't understand their question to mean, "Are you relying on God's power?" *It ought to mean that.*

Sometimes I don't have time for adequate preparation. Emergencies happen. Schedules get changed. And I have learned that when that happens, I need to pray (very earnestly, I might add), *God, I've done what I can to get ready for this. It is in Your hands to use it or not.* Over and over again, those lessons or speaking opportunities or events have turned out more successfully than not. I have learned that it pays to rely on God.

Then there are the other times. My team puts their heart and soul into preparation, and when the time to start comes, we are *ready*. Sometimes, God greatly blesses our efforts. But complete readiness is accompanied by a temptation to forget to depend upon God, because we've got everything under control. I want to make it clear that being ready is more desirable than not being ready, but forgetting to be dependent upon God for power is not. I do it too often. *Shame on me.*

- *Relying on media "wow."* Everything is hi-tech these days. If it isn't, we don't consider it relevant. Let's be honest—the kids aren't the only ones who demand multiple media stimulations to hold their attention. Whatever we present has to be funny or shocking or sad or . . . (you fill it in) or else we're not going to use it. So we spend hours searching the Internet for the right YouTube video or even more time creating our own. When we get it just right, we think we are ready. I know I do that. I can forget that the best media tools can either be a tool of God's power or a distraction from it. *Shame on me.*

- *Relying on manipulative techniques.* I can get kids all hyped up. It's not normally my style, but I know how. And I know some kids' ministry workers who are incredibly good at it. When kids start jumping and cheering and getting emotional, it is sometimes interpreted as God at work. My opinion is "Maybe, but not necessarily." I also know how to give an invitation to kids where I can get virtually every one of them to "raise their hand" for some spiritual decision. But that is something I don't do any more. I am too tired of watching children who "prayed a prayer" in an emotional moment but didn't truly place their faith in Christ. I've learned to do everything I can to help children make life decisions that are genuine. *Good for me.*

Those are not mutually exclusive realms. It *is* possible to be well prepared and still dependent upon God, but it takes discipline—and the right perspective.

So what can we do so the Holy Spirit powers our ministry? Let's go back through the parts of the Power Triangle and discuss implementing them.

Earnest Prayer by Godly People

Getting godly people to pray earnestly for your children's ministry, on a regular basis, is highly desirable but not so easy to make happen. Here are some suggestions.

1. Enculturalize It

What does "enculturalize" mean? It means that we make prayer an expected part of who we are and what we do. When we are talking about praying earnestly, if it is simply *expected*, then it has become part of your culture.

Michael Chanley[1] says that prayer is enculturalized in his church: "I think our team has done a good job with it . . . and it is crucial. Our entire church has made prayer a focus. Having the leadership preach the importance of prayer has a trickle-down effect." In other words, prayer is a part of the culture of Michael's church. Is it a part of yours?

We all understand that it is so much easier to implement something when the whole church (and especially the senior pastor) is talking about it. But what if it is not part of your church culture? Then make it part of the culture of your ministry—the area that you have control over. The next points will tell you how.

Begin by scheduling for earnest prayer. You have to make room for it in your ministry first, and then follow the next three steps:

2. Model It

Prayer must not be an activity that you remember to do, but a behavior that naturally flows from your heart. It has to become your natural reaction to an opportunity to serve. In other words, it must become a habit. Then people must be invited to participate in your habit. If you are going to be successful, you must change your patterns so that your ministry routine demonstrates "earnest prayer by godly people." Evaluate how you spend your time and what you need to adjust so that you have time for prayer—whether it means getting to church earlier, delegating some responsibilities or something else.

3. Expect It

In a discussion on CMConnect about getting volunteers to pray, Aimee Ortega said the following:

> We require that our workers arrive 1 hour early in order to prepare for the class and also to pray before they teach. That is a *requirement*. If not, you will not be ready for the attacks that could come. However, when our volunteers are new, they might not feel like they know how to pray yet. But they are always paired with a more seasoned volunteer that is comfortable with prayer and will pray before class. I like to visit each classroom when I can before service and see if the teachers have already prayed. If they haven't, then I ask to join them in prayer. If teachers are consistently arriving too late to pray and rushing in, their time in the classroom will reflect that. There will be more misbehavior. There will be more of the teacher losing patience. There will be more fruits that do not reflect God. It has to begin in God to show His fruits. If teachers are resistant to that, then perhaps they shouldn't serve in Children's Ministry. And if that continues, then they should not be in your ministry and should be released. If not, God will address you as leader for allowing His movement to be hindered.

One hour early for prayer! That is quite an expectation—and I am sure that God is blessing Aimee's ministry because of it.

Are you too fearful of what might happen if you set such an expectation? Too afraid that people might leave? Then think about the next point.

4. Communicate It

Why do you want to pray anyway? *Because you want God to work.* Compare the following two announcements by a children's ministry leader:

- *Announcement 1:* "We are going to start having a prayer time one-half hour before the service time. I want all of you to be there. I've been feeling like we need to pray, and so I want to implement this prayer time next week."

• *Announcement 2:* "I want more than anything to see God do amazing things in the children we work with. I don't know about you, but I don't know how to make that happen by myself. So . . . I want to try an experiment. The Bible says, *"The earnest prayer of a righteous person has great power and wonderful results."* I am going to start praying earnestly, because I want great power and wonderful results in our ministry. I am asking you to join me. I'm asking you to take an additional step of commitment and see if it is worth it. Beginning next week, I will begin a meeting one-half hour before the service time, and I would like you to join me. I want us to spend 15 minutes in earnest prayer for the kids. I realize that for most of you this will mean adjusting your schedule and getting your family up earlier. But I believe God will honor it. I don't know how, but I believe we will begin to see spiritual power and even more wonderful results."

Yes, announcement #2 is wordier—but that's the point: You must communicate *why* you are implementing prayer, and communicate it effectively.

A Mindset of Weakness

How does one maintain this mindset? Is it something that only comes when circumstances beyond our control press us down and force us into a dependent position? Or is it something we can nurture and grow? I think we can do the latter. Let me explain how.

Challenge Comfort

There is a fine line between competence and comfort. When we know our ministry and can do it with excellence, that is competence. But when we begin to rest upon our competence, that is comfort.

It is usually not wise to challenge competence—in other words, to attempt something for God for which He hasn't equipped us or called us. One of my most frustrating seasons of ministry was when I was working under a man who felt he was called to preach—but he had no competence at all in that role. You've probably experienced a similar situation, and you recognize that serving in a role for which God has given us experience, training and giftedness is best.

But challenging comfort is a different story. Think about this: Can you take your competence (or your team's) and use it to do something that is not so comfortable? What is that something? That's the next point.

Pray for a Cause

Make sure that you can identify what you do in terms of a cause much bigger than you can do in your own strength. I have found that to be so important. The seasons of ministry that have been the most rewarding for me are those in which the mission of what I was undertaking was much larger than I could possibly do.

You can't just say, "Let's do something bigger"; you must start with the cause God puts on your heart. Let that lead you to something that puts you in a position of dependence.

Think of the disciples who listened to Jesus tell them to "disciple all nations" or "preach the gospel to every person" or to be "witnesses to the end of the earth." Those are incredibly huge causes for anyone *today*—even though we have the advantage of global travel, networking and communication—but think how huge they were for the first-century followers of Jesus.

Their heart-and-life commitment to that first cause drove them to attempt some incredible things for God. Think of Thomas, just a common Galilean, who took the gospel to India; or think of Paul, who challenged the best intellectuals of his day in the centers of Greek culture.

This requires you to redefine the norm in terms of the supernatural. What is the cause that is driving the nursery workers in your church? Why do you have VBS or summer camp?

How do *you* define *your* cause? What burns in your soul and drives you to think bigger than what you can possibly handle by yourself? Pray that God will make it clear to you and then enable you to pursue it. You may just see Him do incredible things through you in the process.

Study God's Attributes and God's Heart

The most important thing about me (and you) is how I view God; therefore, the more I study what He is like, the more I will be compelled to rely on Him. The truth is, when I am looking at Him, studying Him, I can do nothing other than be dependent upon Him.

The more I understand Him, the more I will see my trials, adversities and challenges as part of His plan to mature me, or others, and accomplish His purposes.

So when was the last time you studied the attributes of God for yourself?

The Message of the Gospel

No matter how strongly and emphatically we proclaim that we believe in the gospel, there is a temptation to crowd it into a corner of our ministry, out of its rightful place. Maybe that temptation is satanically inspired, or maybe it comes from our own fleshly tendencies, or maybe neither; but it is real for many children's ministry workers. It takes discipline and intentionality to keep the gospel where it belongs—at the core of what we teach and do. Let's think through how we can do that:

How to Keep the Gospel Central

Picture a bicycle wheel and let the spokes represent all the things we must teach children. Let the hub represent the gospel. The spokes are the various doctrines that form foundational truth: Bible stories that inform children about the God's story, godly virtues that guide spiritual formation, and disciplines that lead to godly practices. There are *many* spokes, but there is only one hub—and without it, the spokes are without their anchor that allows the wheel to serve its purpose.

Is the hub—the gospel—central in your content? Is it the core message of your curriculum? Remember, in terms of message, the gospel is the primary source of power for your ministry. It *must* be central, for to treat it as anything less is to fail miserably in grounding children in the Christian faith.

It has been my observation that many children's workers who *say* they believe strongly in the gospel fail to emphasize it in practice. In the previous chapter, I described some of the ways we obscure it, but now I want to share with you what you can do to make sure it stays in its proper place.

- Emphasize the story of the cross in your décor, in your visuals and in your media. I've observed that typically the children's ministry wing of a church is decorated thematically to attract children, not to teach—but even then, messaging that informs and instructs can be included. I've also visited children's ministry areas in churches that have lots of Bible scenes. But in my observation, most of the time the most important scene—the death and resurrection of Jesus—is not usually there. Walk through your children's ministry area. What is portrayed in the decor? Why not portray the gospel? Why not teach and instruct through the permanent visuals you put on the walls?

- Make the memorization of basic salvation verses a staple in your curriculum. Be sure that all of the children under your leadership memorize several core salvation verses—especially John 3:16 and 1 Corinthians 15:3-4. I have found the "gospel wheel" illustration that we use in Awana to be very helpful. It is nonlinear, which means you can start at any point. It is also visual, providing memory triggers for your volunteers to refer to when sharing the gospel. And it is simple, which means that it is easily recalled. Here it is:

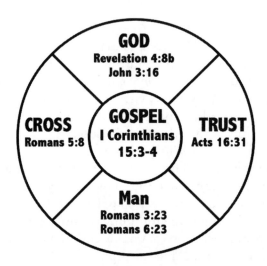

As you can see, the "hub" is the gospel.

The vertical axis is the "nature" axis—reminding us that it is important for a person to know both the nature of *God* and the nature of *man* in order to understand the gospel.

The horizontal axis is the "action" axis. The action of God (the *cross*) is on the left. As He, according to who He is, responds to who we are, we respond back to Him through *trust* (on the right).

You probably have your list of preferred salvation verses. Make it your goal that these verses become deeply embedded into the memory and thinking of the children God has entrusted to you. That means providing visual portrayals of the verses, regular and repeated review and instruction about their meaning.

- *Regularly quiz the children on the core issues of Christianity.* By early elementary age, every child who regularly attends should be familiar with truths that surround the gospel message, such as what the gospel is, what the Bible says we are like on the inside, what God is like (make certain they always mention "He loves me" and "He is holy"), and why Jesus had to die.

- *Speak with wonder and awe about what the gospel means to you.* Remember, you can have a huge impact through your genuine emotion—and you should be showing your emotion over the core message of the gospel.

- *Include the gospel in your teaching and informal conversations with the children.* No matter the topic, connect the gospel message to your discussion. After all, the gospel message is the core of Christianity, so every topic you will teach can be connected to it. When you do so, you elevate its importance in the thinking of the children.

Why do you do this? Not merely because it is the most important message, but also because it is the most powerful one.

Note

1. Michael Chanley is the executive director of International Network of Children's Ministry.

A GOOD DAY OR A GOD DAY?

So, how has your day gone today?

"Good," you respond. That usually means the day presented nothing unusual, nothing catastrophic—everything was pretty much normal. Our best days, however, may not be when things go so smoothly; those days may be God days. What is a God day? When we are dependent upon Him, are disciplined enough to pray earnestly, are engaged with His Word, and are seeking His Spirit's power in our lives.

How about in ministry? Have you had a good year or a God year? Which would you rather have? Which are you praying for?

In this section we have talked about earnest prayer, so take a moment and give some earnest praise to God for a time in which you have seen Him display His power. Enjoy the memory of the greatness of God's work.

Now, ask yourself, "Have I failed to depend upon God like I should in my ministry?" If you need to confess, or pray for guidance, do that. Then enjoy His forgiveness.

Finally, offer praise for the gospel and the spiritual power of it. Thank God for how He has transformed your life through it, and the awesome privilege you have to share it with others.

Earnestly seek to have a God year.

Larry Fowler

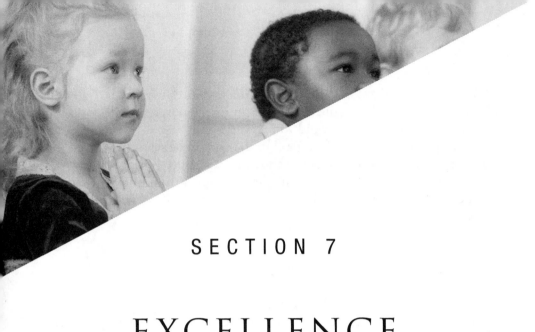

SECTION 7

EXCELLENCE
The Right Quality in Children's Ministry

STANDARD 7:
We carry out our ministry to children with biblical excellence.

Let your light so shine before men, that they may see your good deeds and praise your Father in heaven.
MATTHEW 5:16

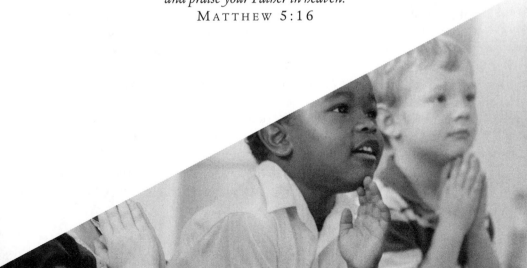

"The Ten Most Excellent Children's Ministries in America." If there really were such a list, who would be on it? Suppose you were on the committee that picked them. What would your criteria be?

Do you think that only large churches would be selected? Would facilities be a consideration? Teacher-child ratio? Budget? Vision?

I don't have a clue about which ministries I would put on the list for America. But if there were a list for the whole world, I'd have a nomination. Let me tell you about it.

Excellence in a Pig Barn

I arrived in Cienfuegos, Cuba after about a three-hour ride from the Havana airport. On the way, my host, Abner Gonzales, told me that a pastor was anxious to meet me. I had come to Cuba because Awana had been launched there about a year before, and my purpose was to assess progress and encourage where I could. It ended up that I was the one who got the encouragement.

After checking in to the hotel, we went to meet the pastor. I don't remember his name, or even his face, but I will not forget his story. After our introductions, he thanked me for bringing children's ministry to his church. As he told me why, the tears began to flow down his face: He had been planting a "mission" (under the Communist government—he wasn't allowed to plant a new church, only a mission of an existing church) and had been struggling terribly to do so in a community marked by hostility, hopelessness and alcoholism.

Then they changed their approach, and started working with the children (an Awana club). In a matter of a few weeks, many children were attending, and then their parents came to see what was going on. The pastor told me of family after family that now were believers and growing in Christ. He said through the interpreter, "You have to come see."

A few days later, Abner took me to see the church and observe their children's ministry. As we drove on the highway, I could see in the distance some quite large buildings that were dome-shaped, like nuclear power plants. I asked Abner what they were. He said, "Those are the plants the Russians were building until you (meaning the U.S.) pressured them into leaving." Not too far away were rows of tall apartment buildings—ugly, square and dirty—like I had seen in my travels in Russia. "That," Abner said, "is Nuclear City [*Ciudad Nuclear*, in Spanish]." The Russians abandoned all of those buildings when they left, and our people have moved in. That is where we are going.

But we didn't go up to the towering apartment buildings. Instead, we drove down a narrow dirt road through a sugarcane field and then pulled through a gate and stopped alongside a small building. It had walls made of cheap concrete block to only about waist-high, then pillars that held up a sheet-metal roof. The upper parts of the walls were open.

It was a pig barn.

Abner and I were greeted by a number of people, and I learned they were the children's workers. They were thrilled by our visit, and anxious to show us what God had been doing.

The pig barn was probably 20 feet wide by 30 feet long. Inside, it had been cleaned up and whitewashed, and there were wooden benches for the children to sit—they were so close together, I wondered if their legs would be able to fit between the rows.

Then the children came inside. And continued to arrive. Parents came, too, but stood outside so the children could be inside. They kept packing in until there were about 100 children. It was wall-to-wall bodies from front to back.

The children sat quietly, waiting to start. *North American kids wouldn't be sitting this still,* I thought.

The workers started with songs. *Wow.* The children sang like nothing I've ever heard in the U.S. That was how the whole meeting went. But my biggest impression wasn't of the children; it was of the workers.

They had *so little.* But they were so dedicated—and creative—and effective. I remember Lorenzo, who was responsible for the activities. He showed me his bag of equipment. He apologized because he didn't have much: he said he wanted to play a game with balls, but they are not available to buy in Cuba, so he had improvised. In his bag were the floats out of toilet tanks, and they played games using them and some sticks!

Another children's worker had organized the mothers to prepare little crafts that the children could complete. Another had made puppets. The one telling the story was an emerging artist, and he had painted his own story visuals on a piece of cardboard. I recall that at the end that they wanted to know how they could improve. I felt completely undeserving of the respect they gave me. I said, "Can I take you with me so that you can show children's workers in North America how to improve?" That probably wasn't the best thing to say in Cuba . . .

Their children's ministry was *excellent.* No matter how you might look at it, in terms of outcome, not only the children, but also whole families were coming to Christ as a result. Their sacrifice was humbling. I found out later they wanted to purchase some children's ministry materials from

Mexico, but rather than ask for a handout, the families of this pig barn church decided they would all eat less for a month. Each family received an allotment of rice from the government, so at the end of the month they would pool their rice together and sell it so they could get the materials they wanted for the children. Their creativity in every area was amazing. They understood discipline and educational development. And their commitment to Christ was so evident.

So where was the cool, attractive décor? The media? The amazing facilities? (Okay, the pig barn was kind of amazing.) It wasn't big, and it didn't evidence any of the cultural standards we might use to qualify excellence. But it was biblically excellent, because biblical excellence is not culturally determined.

Cultural excellence is not bad. In fact, it is necessary for effective ministry. But it is not *primary*. Do you see it that way? Do you put biblical excellence as more desirable than cultural excellence?

Let's find out what it is.

EXCELLENCE IN
THE BIBLE

Studying Excellence

The English word "excellent," or its other forms, such as "excel" or "excellence," is quite rare in the Bible; in fact, according to which translation one uses, it can be found as few as 10 times or up to 46 times.[1] The variation in number is only because some versions tend to use synonyms such as "magnificent" or "great."

What is striking, though, is that in a large majority of cases of the word's use, it refers to God's nature, reputation or work. Here are three examples:

1. God's nature is excellent: *"This also comes from the LORD of hosts; he is wonderful in counsel and excellent in wisdom"* (Isa. 28:29, *ESV*).

2. God's reputation is excellent: *"O LORD, our Lord, how excellent is Your name in all the earth, who have set Your glory above the heavens!"* (Ps. 8:1, *NKJV*).

3. God's work is excellent: *"Praise the LORD in song, for He has done excellent things; let this be known throughout the earth"* (Isa. 12:5, *NASB*).

Rarely is the word "excellent" connected with anything we humans do. The most significant example is found in 1 Corinthians 12:31, in which we are told there is a more excellent way to serve than through spiritual gifts:

> *But eagerly desire the greater gifts. And now I will show you the most excellent way.*

We know what follows: *love*. I will write more about that later.

The scarcity of the word "excellent" regarding our ministry or spiritual service, in our English translations, does not mean the concept is not present in Scripture.

Excellence in the Sermon on the Mount

Jesus set the bar really high for His followers when He said:

> *Let your light shine before men in such a way that they may see your good works, and glorify your Father who is in heaven* (Matt. 5:16, *NASB*).

Let's unpack this. What does "your light" refer to here? It refers to your testimony or your walk with God. Who are "men"? All men—including unbelievers. Who will see your "good works"? The unbelievers. And what else do they do when they see "your light"? They will glorify your Father, who is in heaven.

I've always been awed—and intimidated—by this thought. I would have expected Jesus to say, "that they may see your good works, and *you* glorify your Father who is in heaven." But it's not us who glorify God through our good works (that's a high bar by itself), but the unbelievers that see those good works.

It's like the story of Daniel and his three friends, and the fiery furnace. After they should have been burnt to a crisp, King Nebuchadnezzar who was an unbeliever saw that they were unharmed and said, *"Praise be to the God of Shadrach, Meshach and Abednego"* (Dan. 3:28). What a standard for our testimony! It gives a snapshot of spiritual excellence.

But what IS biblical excellence in ministry? Where are there principles that might guide us—especially in our role as those who work with children? The best place to look, I believe, is in 2 Timothy 1–4.

Excellence in Ministry

Just look at this list of statements that are descriptive of an excellent ministry:

- *"I serve . . . with a clear conscience"* (2 Tim. 1:3).
- *"Join with me in suffering for the gospel"* (v. 8).
- *"I am not ashamed"* (v. 12).
- *"Guard the good deposit that was entrusted to you"* (v. 13).
- *"Be strong in the grace that is in Christ Jesus"* (2:1).
- *"Entrust to reliable men who will also be qualified to teach others"* (v. 2).
- *"Endure hardship with us like a good soldier of Christ Jesus"* (v. 3).
- *"No one serving as a soldier gets involved in civilian affairs"* (v. 4) .
- *"He competes according to the rules"* (v. 5).
- *"I endure everything for the sake of the elect"* (v. 10).
- *"Do your best to present yourself to God as one approved"* (v. 15).
- *"A workman who does not need to be ashamed"* (v. 15).
- *"[A workman] who correctly handles the word of truth"* (v. 15).
- *"Avoid godless chatter"* (v. 16).
- *"Be an instrument for noble purposes, made holy, useful to the Master"* (v. 21).
- *"Prepared to do any good work"* (v. 21).
- *"Flee the evil desires of youth"* (v. 22).
- *"The Lord's servant must not quarrel"* (v. 24).
- *"Be kind to everyone"* (v. 24).
- *"Continue in what you have learned"* (3:14).
- *"From infancy you have known the holy Scriptures"* (v. 15).
- *"So the man of God may be thoroughly equipped for every good work"* (v. 17).
- *"Preach the word"* (4:2).
- *"Be prepared in season and out of season"* (v. 2).
- *"Endure hardship"* (v. 5).
- *"Do the work of an evangelist"* (v. 5).
- *"Discharge all the duties of your ministry"* (v. 5).
- *"I have fought the good fight"* (v. 7).
- *"I have finished the race"* (v. 7).
- *"I have kept the faith"* (v. 7).

You will probably note other phrases. But put them all together and they paint a powerful picture of biblical excellence. There are six phrases, in particular, that are especially appropriate for children's workers. In the next chapter, I will unpack them for you.

Note

1. *King James Version*, 39 times; *New King James Version*, 46 times; *New International Version*, 11 times; *English Standard Version*, 21 times; *New American Standard Bible*, 20 times; *New Living Translation*, 10 times.

MARKS OF BIBLICAL EXCELLENCE

What's wrong with that church? I wondered. I was driving in a different city and passed by a medium-sized church along a four-lane boulevard. One glance told me a lot—the lawn was partly brown and hadn't been mowed in quite a while. There was a message sign in the front, but the letters—which I assumed were supposed to be white—had yellowed. Some letters had fallen down. The parking lot had grass growing up through the cracks in the pavement.

Would you have wondered about the quality of ministry in that church, too? Probably—because you likely come from the same cultural "excellence" viewpoint as I do. But things like grass and signage are not important in a place like Cuba, and no indication at all of effective ministry there.

We must not ignore cultural excellence. That, however, is not my subject for this section—it is *biblical excellence*. Biblical excellence remains constant, no matter the culture, and supersedes cultural norms. Let me share six marks of biblical excellence from 2 Timothy.

A Clear Calling

In 2 Timothy 4:5, Paul writes, *"Discharge all the duties of your ministry."* Not "duties of ministry" or "duties of a ministry"—rather, "duties of *your* ministry." I emphasize the "your" because I believe that Paul assumed an ownership of the ministry on Timothy's part; it was his *calling*. Biblical excellence starts with this—a clear sense of calling.

Question #1: Why am I still here?

Let me ask three questions:

1. "Do you believe heaven will be better than life here on earth?" How do you answer? *Yes?*

2. "Do you believe God wants the best for us?" What do you say? *Yes?*

3. "Then why doesn't He take us directly to heaven?" "Because He has something for us to do here," you say.

So what is that something? Why does God have me—YOU—still here? How strongly your ministry to children links to the answer to that question is the starting point. The reality is, many children's workers are involved in ministry with kids for reasons other than a clear sense of purpose or calling. They are in that position because no one else would volunteer or because a friend pressured them or . . . you know the reasons.

The idea of "calling" was much more glorified a generation or two ago than it is today. In fact, younger volunteers are much more likely to be cause-driven than calling-driven. However, both calling and cause are biblical concepts. I believe that a calling is out of vogue somewhat because of the misuse of the term, not because it is no longer valid. It *is* valid—and vital. If you approach ministry with a clear sense of purpose and calling, you will simply be a much better minister.

Question: What Is a Calling?
My definition is "a definable spiritual purpose for your life." In other words, why you are still here on earth.

Question: What Does God Call People To?
- Sometimes to a lifelong ministry. An example is Paul, who was called to take the gospel to the Gentiles.
- Sometimes to a specific task. Gideon was called to drive the Midianites out of the land.
- Sometimes to a specific place. Jonah was called to Nineveh.

Larry Fowler

Question: How Does God Call People?

God calls people by many different means in the Bible. Some calls were miraculous, some were just normal.

- *Supernatural means:* a burning bush (Moses), angels appearing (Gideon) or God speaking in the night (Samuel).

- *Natural means:* a father's directions (Solomon), a burdened heart (Nehemiah) or a message from a spiritual leader (Saul/Paul—the message from Ananias).

Question: How Can I Know My Calling?

Here are five questions that can help you know God's calling, or purpose, for you at this time in your life:

1. *How would this ministry fit in to God's purpose?* Romans 8:28 tells us we are called according to God's purpose. Can you see God's purpose in this ministry opportunity?

2. *How important do I sense this ministry is?* Philippians 3:14 tells us that our calling is "high" or "lofty." It is not speaking of altitude, but of importance. Has God given you a conviction that this ministry you are doing is highly important?

3. *Do I and others involved have God's peace in our hearts concerning this calling?* Colossians 3:15 tells us that we are called to peace. Note it says, "peace of God," not "peace with God." We receive peace *with* God at the moment of salvation, while peace *of* God accompanies our calling. Has God given you and others who have spiritual input into your life peace about this? Are you and your spouse in agreement?

4. *Do I have the approval of my spiritual leaders?* We see the example in Acts 13:1-3. Spiritual leaders affirmed Paul and Barnabas in their calling. Do your spiritual leaders affirm your calling?

5. *Have I seen God use me in this?* John 15:16 reveals that Jesus said He called us to *"bear fruit—fruit that will last."* Have you seen evidence of that in what you have done?

Single-mindedness

In 2 Timothy 2:4, Paul writes, *"No one serving as a soldier gets involved in civilian affairs."* Suppose I am a private in the army, and I'm addressing my commanding officer: "Sir, I hope you don't mind, but I see an opportunity to make a little money on the side here while I'm in Iraq, so I'm going to set up a little store in the village down the road."

Question #2: How able am I to focus on this ministry?

What would the commanding officer say to that? I'm not going to attempt to write it here. You can guess: Soldiers are expected to be single-focused. Friends, we are in a war, as well, just as Paul references here with Timothy. We will be most effective when we have single-mindedness in ministry.

Roger Vann was a teammate on my college cross-country team at John Brown University. He was one year younger, so when I was a sophomore, he was a freshman. That year, we were pretty much even in running ability. We were the third and fourth best on the team, and sometimes I finished ahead of him, while sometimes he beat me.

The next year, he beat me every race. He became the second-best runner on our team, while I stayed third. My senior year, Roger was awarded small-college All-American status, and in his senior year, after I graduated, he won the National Association of Intercollegiate Athletics small college marathon. I was never better than third on the team. One could argue that Roger was more talented than me, but I'm going to say his success was also due to something else: he was single-minded. Roger was crazy about running. Sometimes he would go out on a Saturday morning and run 40 miles *just for fun.*

In my case, running was just one thing I did in college. I played bass guitar in a music group, sang in the Cathedral Choir, participated in student government and dated Diane. When there was extra time, I fit in a little studying. I was never very good at playing bass. I once ran for student body president and got trampled in a landslide. My grades weren't too great, either—until Diane made me study in order to spend time with her. I enjoyed a lot of things in college, but I never excelled at any (except for catching Diane, which has clearly been the most excellent thing I ever did). Roger, on the other hand, was clearly focused on running, and he became a national champion.

The principle is also true in ministry, isn't it? It is difficult to excel if you are not single-minded. Our ministries are often staffed by willing volunteers who have so many interests and obligations, both at the church and outside of the church, that we get only a small sliver of their time and heart.

These two first points are critical: if we are to have an excellent ministry, we must seek to staff with volunteers who are called of God to do the ministry and can give it a dedicated focus.

Well Prepared

In 2 Timothy 2:21, Paul states that we should be *"prepared to do any good work."* Later, he adds that we should *"be thoroughly equipped for every good work"* (3:17) and *"be prepared in season and out of season"* (4:2).

The ability to get organized and ready with the details of ministry is critical. Some of us have the gift to do it and some of us don't, but nevertheless, it is *essential* to excellence. Good organization is not ministry itself; it is clearing away the obstacles so that effective ministry can take place.

Question #3: How attentive am I to details?

I'm sure you've been on the receiving end of the agony of disorganization. I have:

- The conference director miscalculated the number of lunches needed—by more than 250! That meant there were 250 attendees with growling stomachs that afternoon, which seriously encumbered their ability to learn. It's an understatement to say that it intensified the challenge to keep the attention of those in my workshops.

- I was invited to speak at the final evening VBS session, to which parents were invited. The children's pastor was very emphatic with me—I was to finish *by 8:30 PM*. I was to have 15 minutes to speak, but if things took longer, I was to just speak more briefly and still end at 8:30. However, the transitions between groups of children and their presentations was so disorganized that it wasn't my turn until *9:10 PM!* I just thanked the parents for coming and prayed. I felt that an opportunity for effective ministry was missed because of disorganization.

Let me urge you to be diligent in the details. If it is not your gift, pray for someone who has the spiritual gift of administration to join you in ministry!

To be clear, when Paul was writing this epistle, he was urging Timothy to be *spiritually* prepared in three areas:

1. *Holiness* is the context of 2 Timothy 2. We are to turn away from wickedness (see v. 19) and flee the evil desires of youth (see v. 22). (More about that later.)

2. *Bible knowledge* is the context of 2 Timothy 3. *Scripture is given to us* (see v. 16) so that we can be *thoroughly equipped.*

3. *Mental alertness* is the context of 2 Timothy 4. Be ready to proclaim God's truth is the command. He follows it later in verse 5 with the additional command, *"Keep your head in all situations."*

Being well prepared, whether spiritually or organizationally, is essential to doing our best in serving God.

A Sacrificial Spirit

In 2 Timothy 2:10, Paul states that he endures everything *"for the sake of the elect."* He asks Timothy to *"join with me in suffering for the gospel"* (2 Tim. 1:8) and to *"endure hardship"* (2 Tim. 4:5).

I was in the city of Manaus, Brazil, for a conference. Manaus, situated on the banks of the Amazon River, is an interesting mixture of cultures; rural/jungle exists beside modern/urban. As my plane descended toward the airport, the river itself amazed me, as it looked so wide. I later learned that at Manaus it was five miles wide and averaged 200 feet deep. And that it is 1,000 miles inland—as far as Minneapolis is from where the Mississippi River empties into the Gulf.

My hosts were a family deeply devoted to children's ministry. The third day with them, I learned just how devoted Julio and Carmen and their two teenagers were. They led the Awana ministry in their church, which met on a Friday evening, and it was thriving. They also served together on Sunday morning. But then I learned from others at the conference about their Tuesdays: Both parents took a day off work, and with their two teenagers, they crossed the river in a ferry (one hour). They had a car parked on the other bank. They got in and drove for another hour to a boat landing back in the Amazon jungle. There, they hired a dugout canoe to take them still another hour to a small village on one of the many tributaries, where they taught about 20 children who lived in the village.

Every Tuesday they traveled three hours there, did the Awana ministry and then traveled three hours home . . . as a family. They paid for everything—their own costs, the children's materials—everything.

As I got to know the two teenagers, I could feel their deep commitment to ministry. Their parents were effectively discipling them in their faith. From what I observed, their ministry was *excellent* because of their *sacrifice*.

I tried to think of an American family who did something similar to this family's six hours of travel every week to minister to a small group of children. I could not think of one.

All ministry, if it is to be excellent, must involve sacrifice. However, Christian workers often get confused about what they must sacrifice: Scripture NEVER tells us to sacrifice our children or our marriage. Julio and Carmen included their children in ministry so that it drew them into a life of faith rather than push them away.

In our American Christian culture, we can also err by equating long hours with sacrifice, but that is not what Paul is saying. In the verses sited, he urges Timothy to be willing to sacrifice comfort and ease and even be willing to endure persecution if necessary.

Question #4: What are you willing to sacrifice for ministry?

Are you willing to sacrifice comfort and ease to be effective in ministry?

- Would you skip breakfast in order to attend a prayer meeting of your ministry's workers?

- Would you linger at church in order to connect with a parent, rather than rush home for your football game?

- Would you be willing to spend the time to memorize the verse you're going to tell the kids they should memorize?

Sacrifice. It is a necessity for excellence in ministry.

High Standard of Holiness

In 2 Timothy 1:3, Paul writes, *"I thank God, whom I serve . . . with a clear conscience."* He extols believers to *"turn away from wickedness"* (2 Tim. 2:19) and *"call on the Lord out of a pure heart"* (2 Tim. 2:22).

I am assuming something: among the readers of this book, there will be someone who is careless in his or her Christian walk. Is it you? Are you addicted to something? Is there a secret sin you are harboring? If so, get out. Get out of children's ministry until you have victory.

The failures of a few children's workers in the last two decades have left a putrid stench in the nostrils of so many. Catholic priests are often suspect. Male teachers in elementary schools are sometimes looked upon with wariness just because they are male. The most recent trial garnering national attention of a Penn State football coach is causing all big-brother-type charities to be under extra scrutiny.

When our children were small, we lived in Oxnard, California, and we enjoyed having an orange tree in our backyard. It was a lavish producer of oranges, and we struggled to pick them all when we should. I learned after a while that overripe oranges can look just fine on the outside but be rotten on the inside. I picked many an orange that *looked* excellent, but on the inside they were *worthless*. Our ministry can be like that—we can be like that—if we don't adhere to a high standard of holiness.

How is your standard? Is it high? *There must be no tolerance of the opposite*. If you are missing the mark on this one, either repent and get the help needed to get out of your destructive sin, or else just get out.

Question #5: Am I a godly example?

And while we are on this topic—even if you don't know me, pray for *me*. I have, by God's grace, been able to serve in children's ministry for nearly four decades. I'd like to finish well, so pray that I will maintain a high standard of holiness through the rest of my years of ministry.

Staying Power

At the conclusion to his letter to Timothy, Paul states that he has *"finished the race"* (2 Tim. 4:7), and he tells Timothy to *"Discharge all the duties of your ministry"* (v. 5).

Do you notice the emphasis upon staying power in these two phrases from 2 Timothy 4? Paul urges Timothy to discharge *all* the duties. About himself, he says *I have finished.*

Roger Vann, my college cross-country teammate, whom I mentioned earlier, and I were trying to qualify for the Olympic Trials in the 26-mile marathon. It was the fall of 1975, and we were competing in the Arkansas AAU race, which was a qualifying meet. We, of course, were running against the clock to record a time that would allow us to go to the trials. Roger was a shoo-in, but it would take my all-time best effort for me to make it.

Our team dominated through most of the race: Roger was in first, our teammate Hank Brame was second, and I was in fourth place of about 120 runners. I knew what pace I needed to maintain, and at 20 miles, I was on it and feeling pretty good. I can recall thinking, *I can catch the third runner, and we can finish 1-2-3.* But at 23 miles, I suddenly felt sick—very sick. And after a few steps of trying to go on in spite of it, I did something I had not done in a race before: I stopped. Quit.

I didn't recover quickly. In fact, I was weak and fatigued for a couple of months afterward. The doctor said I had a form of hepatitis, and I ended up on bed rest for that whole time. Of course, I also didn't make the Olympic Trials.

However, at 22 miles, I was doing *excellent.* But no one would call my race excellent, because I didn't finish. You have to finish a race for it to be an excellent one.

I don't want to quit during my spiritual race. At the end of my life, I want to be able to say, with Paul, "I have finished."

I believe our lives are composed of a number of spiritual "races." Sometimes it is a specific involvement in a specific ministry or church. Being a godly parent is a challenging spiritual course. Mentoring a younger person in ministry is a spiritual race.

Question #6: What might cause me to quit?

Are you thinking of quitting a spiritual race? Has God revealed to you, "This race is done—I have a new one for you now"? Or are you dropping out at 23 miles, like I did in the marathon?

If you are going to do your ministry with excellence, you must *finish.*

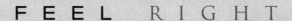

AN AWARD OF EXCELLENCE

There ought to be an award for excellence in children's ministry. But determining the correct criteria likely keeps us from having one. Why? Because the things we can see and measure are not the most important things.

Effective ministry is not measured by the energy and excitement in the kids, by efficient organization, by innovative media or size of ministry or budget. Ministry effectiveness is not even accurately measured by how many kids profess Christ (do we know for sure what goes on in the heart?), or by progress in Bible knowledge or understanding.

As difficult as it is to determine the criteria, I still think there ought to be an award for excellence. *Wait:* there IS! There is an award coming your way for excellence in ministry. Paul talked about it in 1 Corinthians 3:10-14:

> *By the grace God has given me, I laid a foundation as an expert builder, and someone else is building on it. But each one should be careful how he builds. For no one can lay any foundation other than the one already laid, which is Jesus Christ. If any man builds on this foundation using gold, silver, costly stones, wood, hay or straw, his work will be shown for what it is, because the Day will bring it to light. It will be revealed with fire, and the fire will test the quality of each man's work. If what he has built survives, he will receive his reward.*

Larry Fowler

The reward for excellence in ministry is coming. Few of us will ever get one here on earth, but someday we will get a better one than we could ever get here. *A far better award.* Let's be excellent—biblically speaking—in all that we do, and remember that eternal reward.

How does that make you feel?

ROCK-SOLID STANDARDS

Standard 1
We target the hearts of the children.

Standard 2
We reflect the nature and work of God in every discipline situation.

Standard 3
We value both approaches—mothering and fathering—
in spiritual discipleship.

Standard 4
We are locked on to the needs of children and the desired
spiritual outcome in their lives.

Standard 5
We value every individual child and are concerned about not
losing even one.

Standard 6
We know where spiritual power comes from and rely upon it to
fuel our ministry.

Standard 7
We carry out our ministry to children with biblical excellence.

Larry Fowler

DISCUSSION GUIDE

Section 1: Bull's-eye
The Target of Children's Ministry

Think Right: Targeting the Heart of a Child

1. What verses can you find (or think of) that reference the heart? In those verses, what do you think the term "heart" refers to?
2. What do you believe the "heart" means, figuratively speaking, in our culture? Can you give an example?
3. Look at the illustration "Three Meanings of 'Heart'" found on page 24. React to how the Bible's usage of "heart" differs from the cultural usage.
4. "It is the heart of a child that counts. Targeting anything less is inadequate." Do you agree with this statement? Why or why not?
5. Review Philippians 4:8-9, the scriptural foundation for the discipleship process. (You may want to look again at page 26.) Why is this sequence so important?
6. Think about the three emphases from the recent history of children's ministry. What have you observed from your experience as the target—"Bible knowledge," "practical application," or "relevance"? What makes you draw that conclusion?
7. What is inadequate about simply targeting Bible knowledge?
8. Describe the relationship between "gaining Bible knowledge" and "thinking" (the biblical "heart").
9. What is inadequate about simply emphasizing practical application?
10. How can practical application impact a child's heart?
11. What are the pitfalls of simply targeting relevance?
12. How does relevance relate to how a child thinks?
13. Is it possible to maintain one (or all) of those as a target but have the heart of the children as the bull's-eye?

Do Right: Seven Ways to Impact Thinking
Introduction

1. Give an example of something or someone that deeply impacted your thinking as a child, and why you think it had such an impact.

Modeling
1. Do you agree with the statement, "More than any other single factor, thinking is molded by modeling"? Why or why not?
2. Think of co-workers who effectively "model" for the children. What do they do that causes you to think of them?
3. In your role in children's ministry, what are a couple of your greatest obstacles to modeling your faith in front of your students?
4. How are modeling and strong relationships related? What impact might that have on your role in your children's ministry?

Testing
1. Recall a time when your thinking was altered through a test. You may need to refer back to the chapter if you need refreshing about the meaning of "test" in this context.
2. Think back to the last lesson you participated in. What was the application? Were the children "told," or were they challenged to test the Bible truth?
3. What can a child do in your ministry to exercise his or her faith? Do you need to create opportunities for the children to do so or not?
4. If you need to create opportunities, brainstorm ideas about what kinds of service responsibilities, events or outings you could create so kids can "test" their faith for themselves.

Emotions
1. Can you think of a time when your heart has been impacted by another person's emotions—either positively or negatively? Share it if you feel comfortable doing so.
2. Think back to the last time you saw emotion shared in your children's ministry by an adult worker. What was the reason for the emotion?
3. Was the impact of the worker's efforts to minister changed because of the emotion? Why do you say that?
4. Think of something you might show positive emotion about in your children's ministry: it might be joy, excitement, awe—but decide what you could do to impact children more through emotions.

Repetition
1. Think of something that is deeply embedded in your thinking because of repetition. What is it?
2. How many times should one repeat a truth or concept so that it impacts the thinking of children?

3. Do you think repetition of core biblical truth is intentional or by chance in your children's ministry? What would you point to as evidence that supports your opinion?
4. How could you better build repetition into your ministry? Try to think of several ways.

Questions
1. What is your tendency? Are you more of a question-asker or an advice-giver?
2. Have you experienced a time when the children got so involved in learning that they started asking questions of you? What was it like?
3. Would you say there is ample opportunity for children to ask questions in your children's ministry?
4. How could you better use the technique of asking questions as part of your ministry?

Consistency
1. Think about those who have impacted your thinking. Were you impacted by consistency of message or inconsistency?
2. Why is consistency so important to a child?

Section 2: Reconciliation
Discipline in Children's Ministry

Think Right: God's Economy of Discipline
1. Can you recall the six elements in God's economy of discipline?
2. What strikes you as significant about what you read about how God punishes?
3. What is God's purpose in punishment?
4. What, in your observation of parents in general, do you find to be the contrast between God's purpose and the norm of parental purpose in punishment?
5. Why is the element of God's forgiveness so amazing?
6. Do you agree with the book's definition of reconciliation?
7. How often do you think parents complete the process of discipline and bring it to the point of reconciliation?
8. Why—spiritually speaking—is the word "reconciliation" a good summary of any ministry?

Do Right: Mirroring God in Discipline

1. React to this statement from the chapter: "The most opportune time to teach children about the nature of God is when you discipline."
2. What elements of discipline in your children's ministry are spelled out specifically? Clear rules? Consequences? Different techniques for crowd control and individual rebellion? Guidelines for reconciliation?
3. React to *Element 2: A Child Sins*. How do you think parents do in mirroring God in this element?
4. What is the difference between just getting the wrong behavior to stop, and repentance? Why is repentance so much more desirable?
5. Why is getting a child to say "sorry" not enough?
6. How do you get a child to repent?
7. What in your experience is a barrier to completing this element in the discipline process?
8. Think of the most recent discipline opportunity you've had in children's ministry. Did reconciliation take place? What would it have looked like, if it didn't take place?

Section 3: Gender Balance
The Workers of Children's Ministry

Think Right: Fatherlessness in the Church

1. What is your personal experience or observation about the importance of fathering?
2. What is your reaction to the Swiss study referenced in the section under the subhead, "We Need Men in Our Churches"?
3. Are men in a minority in your children's ministry? What would you estimate the percentage to be?
4. Can you restate the argument in your own words about fathering and mothering as activities of God?
5. Why is the mothering activity of the biblical God unique as a concept of God?
6. Look at Ephesians 6:4. How can you explain the difference between the two words that are translated "nurture" and "admonition" in the *KJV* translation?
7. How did the apostle Paul use both the mothering approach and the fathering approach in discipling the new believers in Thessalonica?
8. How would you describe mothering as a discipleship activity in children's ministry?

9. How would you describe fathering as a discipleship activity in children's ministry?

10. How would you assess the balance in your children's ministry?

Do Right: Gender Balance in Children's Ministry

1. Is a better balance between fathering and mothering approaches desirable for your ministry? Would a solution in your situation be to recruit and retain more men?

2. What recruitment pleas have you heard in the past regarding children's ministry—from the pulpit of your church or otherwise?

3. Does your children's ministry have a vision statement? If so, does it sound more like mothering, fathering or a balance, in your opinion?

4. Read the U.S. Marines recruiting statement and analyze it. Why is it so attractive to young men? Through it, what learning can you discover about recruiting men to your children's ministry?

5. How would you define the unique contribution men can make in children's ministry?

6. Look again at the diagram in the section "Think Mt. Whitney" (see page 89). Explain what is meant by a "low-threat entry point" and a "big challenge."

7. Think through your children's ministry worker policies. Are there some that might make men uncomfortable? If so, can you think of how the policy might be altered to accomplish the same goal but not deter men from serving in children's ministry?

8. Assess your décor. Is it man-friendly?

9. Describe the entry positions for new workers in your children's ministry. Are there sufficient *activity* entry points for men?

10. Assess your ministry structure. Are men serving shoulder-to-shoulder? What is meant by that term?

11. What do you think about the statement, "They [men] *love* to compete?" How can you take advantage of that in recruiting and retaining men in children's ministry?

Section 4: Double Vision
The Right Focus of Children's Ministry

Think Right: The Two Lenses of Children's Ministry

1. What part of the story about Peter and John and the beggar at the gate especially impresses you? What is your takeaway from the story?

2. Can you think of other stories in the Bible where we see a focus on the need of a person?
3. Why did Nehemiah go to Jerusalem, according to this chapter? How might this point focus your children's ministry?
4. Can you think of other stories in the Bible where we see a focus on the spiritual outcome?
5. What does the author mean in this chapter by "double vision"? Why is having this "double vision" helpful to a children's ministry worker?
6. Think back to the last few weeks of your ministry to kids. What was your focus—your vision—on?

Do Right: How to Get Your Ministry in Focus

1. How many children do you personally work with in children's ministry? On a scale of 1 to 10, how well do you know their needs?
2. Look at the sample chart in the section "Children's Needs in Clear Focus." Which column is the most difficult for you to fill out about the children to whom you minister?
3. What does it mean to you, in your situation, to not be "distracted by the Beautiful Gate?"
4. What is the difference between a global vision and a numbers focus?
5. What might be the danger in a numbers focus?
6. What do you want to be able to say about your children (either your own, or those you minister to) when they are age 30?
7. How should the answer to the above question guide your ministry choices in the next year?
8. Look again at the "Focus Failure" section, with its examples. Can you think of a time when you have personally experienced—or observed—focus failure?

Section 5: The Significant "One"
The Right Organization of Children's Ministry

Think Right: Jesus and the Significance of One

1. How do you react to the serious warning of Matthew 18:6?
2. Can you identify the child or children in your ministry that workers are tempted to despise? How are you helping one another have a correct attitude toward that child?

3. Retell the story of the 100 sheep in your words, as "if Jesus were like us here at our church."
4. Do you think your children's ministry is more concerned about the 99, or the one? Why do you have that opinion?
5. Why do you think "one" was such a prominent number in this teaching by Jesus (see Matt. 18:1-14)?
6. How would you define "wandering away?"
7. What story can you identify that emphasizes the potential of a child?
8. Do you believe that most of the workers in your children's ministry stay alert to the potential of the children they are ministering to? Why or why not?

Do Right: Organizing for Retention
1. How well do you personally understand your child registration process?
2. Are you confident that you are gathering the essential, adequate information on *each* child? What is that information?
3. How do you track absenteeism?
4. What specifically do you do to encourage a child who has been absent to come back?
5. Do you use the recordkeeping in place to evaluate ministry effectiveness? How could you do that better?
6. Are you confident that every child in your group is receiving quality individual attention? If not, what could you do to improve the structure so that it becomes possible?
7. Do your volunteers see themselves as shepherds? What leads you to believe this?
8. React to the two basic shepherding principles. Are they a reality in your ministry?

Section 6: Power Triangle
The Right Power in Children's Ministry

Think Right: Spiritually Powered Ministry
1. What, in your opinion, was the most significant point in this chapter?
2. Do you agree or disagree with the statement, "the temptation to forget to depend upon God for power is huge in children's ministry?" Why or why not?

3. How often does your children's ministry team pray together? What percentage of your children's workers participate in the prayer time?
4. If you do pray together, would you characterize the prayer time as "earnest prayer"? Explain your answer.
5. Can you think of a time and/or place when your ministry team could pray more consistently and earnestly?
6. What do you think the results might be if you, as a team, were devoted to more earnest prayer?
7. Would you say that you and your ministry team members are in a "position of weakness"? In other words, a position where you have no choice but to depend upon God? Why or why not?
8. How often, in your estimation, do you think the simple gospel message of 1 Corinthians 15:3-4 is communicated to children?
9. In your judgment, is that often enough—and is it emphasized enough—to be seen as *core* by both the children and the adult volunteers?
10. Look at the section under the subhead, "We Blow it." Which of those failures have you observed in your experience?
11. How do you stay dependent upon the Holy Spirit for spiritual power?

Do Right: The Path to Power

1. Can you identify with any of the four "relying on" statements at the beginning of this chapter? Which one(s), and why?
2. What does it mean to "enculturalize" earnest prayer?
3. Do you think others would say you model earnest prayer? How could you improve your "modeling"?
4. Is getting together for prayer an expectation in your program? Do you think it could be? Why or why not?
5. Analyze Announcement #2 under the subhead "Communicate It." What strikes you as noteworthy in how this announcement is worded?
6. Why is being comfortable in our ministry role an impediment to God's power at work?
7. How do you define your ministry "cause"?
8. Explain the axis of the "gospel wheel."
9. Which "salvation verses" do you prefer to use when explaining the gospel to a child?
10. When the gospel is spoken of in your children's ministry, what do you think the teacher's normal voice inflections and body language tell the children about its importance?
11. Did you discover two significant reasons why the gospel should remain the core message of your ministry?

Section 7: Excellence
The Right Quality in Children's Ministry

Think Right: Excellence in the Bible
1. What did you learn about the use of the word "excellence" in the Bible?
2. Explain how the concept of excellence is found in Matthew 5:16.
3. What phrases from 2 Timothy strike you as especially indicative of a standard of excellence?
4. How would you differentiate *biblical* excellence from *cultural* excellence?

Do Right: Marks of Biblical Excellence
Calling
1. How do you react to the definition of a calling: "A definable spiritual purpose for your life"?
2. Can you identify a spiritual purpose for your life? If so, what is it?
3. How does what you are doing in ministry relate to that spiritual calling or purpose?
4. Of the five points that follow the question, "How can I know my calling?" which one strikes you as most significant in your situation? Why?

Single-mindedness
1. Explain the point of 2 Timothy 2:4 in your own words.
2. What do you see as the greatest obstacles to single-mindedness among children's workers?
3. Think of someone whom you believe is single-minded. What are the positive benefits of being single-minded that you observe in his or her life?
4. How can you encourage the volunteers in your ministry to be more single-minded?

Well Prepared
1. The meaning of the verses cited in this part (2 Timothy 2:21; 3:17; 4:2) is spiritual preparedness. How can a person get spiritually prepared for the ministry role that you have?
2. How does organizational preparedness pave the way for effective ministry?
3. What is the greatest challenge your ministry faces in being organizationally prepared? Take some time to also think of a solution.
4. Who, in your opinion, is a great example of spiritual preparedness? Explain what it is about them that gives you that opinion.

A Sacrificial Spirit
1. Can you think of a co-worker who exemplifies a sacrificial spirit? What do you think motivates him or her to give so much?
2. Why don't some children's workers have a sacrificial spirit?
3. What do you think a sacrificial spirit looks like in your ministry?
4. What does one do to cultivate a sacrificial spirit?

High Standard of Holiness
1. How do you think Paul was able to say in 2 Timothy 1:3, *"I thank God, whom I serve . . . with a clear conscience"*? What does it take to have a clear conscience?
2. What should a children's worker do who is struggling with a sinful pattern in his or her life?
3. What should the standard of holiness be for a children's worker? Give your best shot at defining what we should expect.
4. If one children's worker is aware that another is not maintaining an acceptable standard in his or her life, what should the first worker do?

Staying Power
1. What do you think the apostle Paul meant when he said, *"I have finished the race"* (2 Tim. 4:7)?
2. When should a person quit a ministry?
3. What are some of the benefits of long-term involvement in a specific ministry?
4. What is the most significant thing you have learned in this whole section about biblical excellence?

ABOUT LARRY FOWLER

Larry Fowler serves as executive director of global networking for Awana and KidzMatter. Both organizations are committed to helping churches and parents raise children and youth to know, love and serve Jesus Christ. For more than 30 years, Larry has pursued this mission in a range of capacities, including local-church Awana volunteer, missionary, speaker, author, teacher and executive director of international ministries, program development and training.

The International Network of Children's Ministry (INCM) recently presented Larry with its Legacy Award for 30 years of service in children's ministry. Larry accepted the award from INCM Executive Director Michael Chanley at the Children's Pastors' Conference in San Diego on February 29, 2012.

Larry's Story

Since age 13, when he first sensed God's calling on his life, Larry has exhibited passion and commitment to children's and youth ministry. After graduating with a Master's Degree in Christian Education from Talbot Theological Seminary, Larry served as youth pastor at a church in southern California.

Larry was introduced to Awana as part of a student project he completed at seminary. He was instantly drawn to the ministry's commitment to evangelism and discipleship through Bible memory, a discipline his parents had instilled in him as a child. Shortly after his appointment as youth pastor, Larry started Awana in that church.

As he witnessed Awana bringing kids to Christ and growing his church, Larry's involvement with Awana grew. Awana sees our own country as a mission field. Larry became a full-time Awana missionary in 1979, serving churches and starting Awana programs in the Los Angeles area until 1996.

During that time, he also played a pivotal role in launching Awana in Russia after the collapse of communism. Today, Awana programs operate in more than 400 churches and orphanages throughout the former Soviet Union. This experience ignited Larry's desire for international ministry. It also fueled his passion for training and equipping leaders to work with children. Leaving California to join Awana headquarters in 1996, Larry used his extensive experience in the field to begin training other missionaries, both in the U.S. and internationally. Having trained children's workers in 45 countries, Larry is a key influencer of children's ministries around the world.

Larry is an author of four books—*Rock-Solid Children's Ministry, Rock-Solid Volunteers, Raising a Modern-Day Joseph* and *Rock-Solid Kids*—and a speaker to audiences worldwide both inside and outside of Awana. He is also a recognized expert in issues facing families and churches in the twenty-first century.

A Voice on the Crisis Facing Today's Families

Larry is a leading voice sounding the alarm about a rising epidemic among our youth. Research shows that, despite being raised in Christian homes, attending church regularly and participating in youth group, the majority of U.S. teens leave the church after high school.

"The spiritual goals we have for our youth are failing," Larry says. "Parents need to stop delegating the spiritual training of their children and take a more active role. Churches and families need a clear target, a plan of action and a collaborative strategy to grow spiritually strong kids."

Larry's book *Raising a Modern-Day Joseph* (David C. Cook, 2008), addresses these very issues. Based on Joseph of the Old Testament, it offers a biblical plan for developing children and youth into faithful, Christ-following adults.

Rock-Solid Volunteers reveals timeless principles for recruiting and retaining volunteers in the church.

Raising a Modern-Day Joseph follows Larry's first book, *Rock-Solid Kids* (Gospel Light), which focuses on the need for churches and parents to build a healthy children's ministry modeled on biblical teaching.

An Advocate for the Family

Larry knows firsthand the defining impact parents can make on their children's spiritual lives. Living on a cattle ranch in the rural West, Larry's parents embraced the responsibility of leading their kids' spiritual development. They consistently taught Scripture to their children and helped them memorize, learn and apply it to life. They also modeled Christ for their kids. In fact, Larry's 95-year-old mother taught two Bible studies until just recently.

"My parents were by far the greatest influence on my walk with Christ," Larry says.

The legacy of Larry's parents continues today. "Everyone in my extended family is a Christian," Larry says. "It all started with my parents and their commitment to raising their children to know, love and serve Christ."

A Speaker for Parents and Churches

Larry has served as a keynote speaker and workshop teacher at churches and conferences around the world. Larry addresses a variety of topics, primarily:

- How churches and parents can—and need—to work together to raise spiritual champions
- The important role youth and children's ministry play in the life of a church
- How parents can build a lasting foundation of faith in their children

Larry has also been featured on radio, including Moody's *Prime Time America*. He is also a regular contributor for Focus on the Family and a frequent Christian radio guest. He and his wife, Diane, have two grown children and five grandchildren. The Fowlers reside in Riverside, California.

How to Contact Larry

To schedule an interview, contact David Bunker at 630-540-4695, or email mediarelations@awana.org.

A BIBLICAL FOUNDATION FOR TEACHING
CHILDREN

Rock-Solid Kids
Larry Fowler
ISBN 978-0-8307-3713-0
ISBN 0-8307-3713-8

Sometimes children are viewed in terms of their future value. But to Jesus, children were precious in the here and now, and He gave them His full attention and love. We must view children in the same way and make certain that the way in which we teach children is based on what ought to be the most important influence—the Word of God. Whether your children's ministry is in your home or in your church, *Rock-Solid Kids* will help you build a strong ministry modeled on scriptural teaching. This unique examination of the biblical basis for children's ministry includes eight core chapters. Each chapter is based on one or more Scripture passages and covers topics such as the importance, responsibility, content and golden opportunity of children's ministry. The "foundation rocks" in this book are exactly what teachers and parents need to help them develop a set of convictions—based solidly on the Word of God—for teaching children about Christ.

THE FOUNDATION OF ROCK-SOLID MINISTRY IS

VOLUNTEERS

Rock-Solid Volunteers
Larry Fowler
ISBN 978-0-8307-5745-9
ISBN 0-8307-5745-7

How can you keep volunteer workers engaged in ministry that will change lives? If you struggle to attract long-term volunteers, you're not alone. Pastors, children's pastors and ministry leaders consistently point to recruiting and retaining dedicated volunteers as one of their biggest challenges. Larry Fowler believes that there are seven biblical principles, drawn from the book of Nehemiah, that will help you more effectively motivate and manage volunteers. *Rock-Solid Volunteers* looks at the obstacles Nehemiah and his volunteer workers faced—including fatigue, weakness, loss of vision, peer pressure and opposition—and examines the seven steps Nehemiah took to lead his team to success. Using the principles you'll discover inside, you can attract, inspire and keep talented, committed volunteers, no matter the challenge!